ABOUT MEN & WOMEN

How Your "Great Story"
Shapes Your Destiny

tad guzie · noreen monroe guzie

Paulist Press
New York/Mahwah

The publisher gratefully acknowledges the use of the lyrics from "Suzanne," words and music by Leonard Cohen, copyright © 1966 by Project Seven Music, a division of Continental Total Media Project, Inc., 10 Mitchell Place, White Plains, N.Y.

Library of Congress Cataloging-in-Publication Data

Guzie, Tad W.
      About men and women.

      Includes bibliographies.
      1. Interpersonal relations.   2. Women—Psychology.
3. Men—Psychology.   4. Archetype (Psychology).
5. Sex role.   I. Guzie, Noreen Monroe.   II. Title.
HM132.G89   1986   305.3   86-8747
ISBN 0-8091-2813-6 (pbk.)

Published by Paulist Press
997 Macarthur Boulevard
Mahwah, New Jersey 07430

Printed and bound in the
United States of America

Contents

Acknowledgments

We are grateful to our friends who have given beauty to this book with their calligraphic interpretations of what we have written: Meg Van Rosendaal (Mother), Patti Dawkins (Companion), Gail Stevens (Amazon), Betty Locke (Mediatrix), Gaye Mackie (Father), Renate Worthington (Seeker), Reg Sauvé (Warrior), Jill Pollock (Sage), Marian Peterson (definition of archetypes), and Leslie-Ann Drummond (type and archetype). The Celtic knots and symbols were done by Denice Thibault, with acknowledgment to George Bain. Noreen Guzie did the dedication page and chapter titles.

aine · gary francis ·
cliff caplette · mary
walchuck · len hag
bar...

to the men and women
whose lives are part of this book

ford · john sinnwe
margaret bensette ·
le · ray sevigny · al
cindy garneau · ste
dicastri · leo klug ·
orna bridarolli · ja
glenn mitchell · ma
ey · nobuyasu kira
sandy ens · merika
er grace · michael
leanne dunne · joe
mae stolte · david
mchugh · theresa n

1

ARCHETYPES ·
THE GREAT STORIES

Monica longs for a better relationship with her older sister. They have much in common, yet they are barely on speaking terms. Monica and Karen live in the same neighborhood and are only two years apart in age. They both have three children and degrees in education. There has been tension in their relationship ever since they were children. Monica feels much closer to her other sister Barbara, who is single and ten years her junior. With little effort there has always been mutual understanding.

Tom sees himself as a responsible, caring person. Yet he cannot define duty and responsibility as his father does. Tom acknowledges that his father means well, but there has always been friction in the relationship. Now that he is an adult, it does not bother him anymore that his dad seems to favor Tom's younger brother. But Tom hopes that someday his father will recognize his endeavors as worthwhile. He realizes that his father's attitude toward him has nothing to do with his being a member of the younger generation. In fact, Tom's values are personified in his grandfather. He feels challenged yet comfortable with his grandfather and experiences him as a kindred spirit.

Why do we spontaneously feel an affinity toward one person, and aversion toward another? Why does a parent favor one child over another? Why do children from the same family make such diverse life choices? Why is the most unlikely person a kindred spirit to us, while those whom we are obliged to love annoy us with the best of intentions? How can I understand and love others better?

This book will answer these questions with practical insights.

Walk into any bookstore, and your attention is bound to be caught by a whole section of books that explain how you can become a more fulfilled person in any imaginable circumstance: How to cope with marriage, divorce, and changing relationships. How to parent and how to stepparent. How to be successfully single. Even how to be a good mistress.

This section of self-help books didn't exist a generation ago. People weren't all that different in the past, but they didn't talk about the dynamics of human relationships the way we do now. Look at the old movies on the Late Show. Pretty simple and straightforward fare. Boy meets girl, boy loses girl, boy gets girl. There are no subtleties in their relationship, but still the plot spells out absolutely everything about their ups and downs. The movie is slow, slow, slow. It assumes that the viewer is utterly unsophisticated about how people interact. Today's TV soaps are sexually graphic in ways that the old movies could not be. But even the soaps allow us to draw some of our own conclusions about the real reasons why Marge and Harry broke up.

A certain degree of self-awareness and self-understanding is taken for granted today—in movies, on TV, in literature. It is interesting to see how popular literature dealing with man-woman relationships has changed over the past few generations. Before the twentieth century, people's attitudes toward the relationships between men and women centered around stories about marriage. These stories were expressed in myths that go back to ancient oral traditions and to popular legends that made their way into the fairy tales of every ethnic group. These old stories—Greek and Roman, Teutonic, Celtic, Nordic—reflect the collective understanding of ordinary people, "just folks."

The stories about man-woman relationships are all quite similar. They end when a young man and a young woman (they always seem to be young and vigorous) have overcome the obstacles that stand in the way of their getting married. It is assumed that they "live happily ever after." The old tales are not interested in the "ever after." Whatever happens once the woman and man have overcome the hindrances to a conventional sexual union is not interesting enough to be recorded. Even as late as the nineteenth century, stories like *Jane Eyre* or the novels of Charles Dickens show no change in this pattern. It is only in our century that popular literature gets interested in what happens to the couple *after* their nuptials. This represents a substantial growth in consciousness regarding man-woman relationships.[1]

Certainly the problems of married couples were always there. There were labels for the wife who was a shrew, a bitch, or a harlot. There were labels for the husband who was a tyrant, a womanizer, a drunkard, or an ineffectual cuckold. We only need to read Chaucer, Shakespeare, or Richard Sheridan to pick up all these stereotypes. The single life was not a recognized lifestyle. Books and plays contained maiden aunts, spinsters, and eccentric bachelors. But unless you were a nun or a priest, being single meant that through force of circumstance you never had the good fortune to marry.

Until our own time, myth and folk tales and popular literature did not usually penetrate *beyond* the labels. The problems of marriage were stereotypical: being married to a shrewish wife or a tyrannical husband. Deeper questions dealing with growth, self-discovery, or any of the things that have to do with a real relationship between a man and a woman were rarely recorded in literature or plays.

This means that people would not have had an effective *language* for dealing with the normal struggles that come after the wedding. "My husband/my wife doesn't understand me" is very modern language which we don't generally find in literature before the twentieth century. Before our time, people lacked a common language, a common narrative structure, for talking to others about their on-going relationship. To put it very concretely, I couldn't talk to you about how my wife doesn't understand me. And even if I could put this accurately into words—which would have been difficult, because there was no common language for it—I couldn't hope that *you* would understand me.

In the twentieth century, on the other hand, the struggles of man and woman have become a public part of the human story. From novels to TV dramas and comedies, people have been given a public language—a common narrative structure—for dealing with the dynamics of man-woman relationships. We now see these struggles as a natural and integral part of the fabric of marriage, not odd or comic or unusual exceptions to an abstractly ideal relationship. We have also come to see the single life as a legitimate lifestyle that extends beyond convents and monasteries.

In short, we are living with new forms of self-awareness, new ways of dealing with the masculine and the feminine, new understandings of what it is to be male and female. This is why there are so many books on the bookstore shelves which weren't there a few decades ago. This is also why we are bored today with movies that everyone enjoyed a generation ago.

All of this is quite new. Today there is a proliferation of books on human relationships and personal growth. But if you do some arithmetic on books for men and books for women, you will find that there are far more self-help materials for women than for men. The title we have chosen for this book, *About Men and Women*, reflects our interest in redressing this imbalance. Men and women are equally represented in the pages that follow. We are convinced that it is not possible to understand the psychological orientation of women without referring to parallels in men, and vice versa.

The general approach we are taking in this book has its foundations in the thought of Carl Jung and other writers who have been inspired by his work. Readers who are acquainted with Jungian literature will recognize some familiar themes. But we do not expect on the part of our readers any previous exposure to Jungian theory. The only thing you need to bring to this book is your own lived experience.

This book is about the Great Stories that men and women

have been living from time immemorial, in every era and in every culture. These are the names of the Great Stories:

	MOTHER	FATHER	
AMAZON	MEDIATRIX	WARRIOR	SAGE
	COMPANION	SEEKER	

There are four feminine stories and four masculine stories. Each of these is a Great Story in the sense that men and women in every era have found their identity and fulfillment in living one or two of these stories. Our personal strengths, abilities, instincts, deficiencies, priorities and values all flow from the Great Stories that we live. The next two chapters will tell the Great Stories in detail and explain what each of the names in the diagram means. The arrangement of the names in the diagram is also important, and that will become clear as the book proceeds.

Throughout the book, we will be using the word *archetype* as a synonym for Great Story. *Arche* in Greek means something that is basic, original, or bottom-line. *Typos* means something that makes an imprint. The eight Great Stories are "archetypes." They are ancient, primordial images that are impressed on the human psyche, yours and mine, as a result of the age-long experience of life that has existed before you and I appeared on the scene.

The archetypes are primarily names for psychological realities, but they are also connected with the human physical organism. Anthony Stevens, in an exciting study which relates Jungian theory to the biological sciences, defines archetypes as "innate neuropsychic centers possessing the capacity to initiate, control and mediate the common behavioral characteristics and typical experiences of all human beings irrespective of race, culture or creed."[2] This definition suggests, as Jung himself suggested, that there are as many archetypes as there are general situations in life. In this book, we are confining our use of the word to the eight Great Stories given in the diagram above.

Scholars have used a variety of names for the Great Stories. We have settled on the names we have given in the diagram because they speak to the average person, and at the same time they preserve a classical flavor. We have consulted the research that has been done on archetypes.[3] But our book is mainly based on our own work with several thousand people. These are men and women whom we have met in courses and workshops we have given throughout North America since 1981. We have worked with people of all ages, from all economic brackets, with varying levels of education, and from a variety of cultural backgrounds.

Each of the "archetypes" that we will talk about refers to a pattern of psychic energy, a way of life, a way of being and becoming a fulfilled human person. The archetypes are a large part of our collective human history, perhaps the largest part. The Great Stories transcend you and me, your personal story and mine. At the same time, these age-old stories help to explain why you and I have lived the way we have lived, and why we have made the choices we have made.

Understanding your archetype is a way of understanding who you are and who you are not. Understanding your archetype will tell you a great deal about how you relate to other women, other men, your parents, your children, your peers. Understanding your archetype explains how you receive other people, and how others receive you. Your archetype will tell you about loving, about parenting, and even about your way of conducting business. Marriage, the single life, midlife and old age are all affected by the Great Stories we live.

Archetypes explain the irrational attraction we sometimes have to other people, and the illogical dislike we experience when meeting someone for the first time. Often we know our own story only too well. I am the hero or heroine of my own story, and that is as it should be. But I need to recognize and appreciate that there are Great Stories other than the one I live, and other ways than my way to be heroic.

Read the Great Stories in the next two chapters. You will enjoy seeing yourself and your relatives and friends in them. After the basic descriptions of the eight archetypes, we will talk about the different ways that people live the Great Stories, and how the stories interact with one another.

Notes

1. M. Esther Harding, *The Way of All Women* (Harper Colophon, 1970), pp 279–282.
2. Anthony Stevens, *Archetypes* (Quill, 1983), p 296.
3. Toni Wolff was the first to write about the four feminine archetypes in a brief paper published by the Jung Institute in Zurich, 1956 *(Structural Forms of the Feminine Psyche)*. Her work has been embellished by various Jungian analysts, most recently in an unpublished doctoral dissertation by Pamela S. Stevenson (*Wolff's Four Forms of the Feminine Psyche: Toward a Clinical Application*, California School of Professional Psychology in Berkeley, 1983). Very little has been written on the parallel masculine archetypes. Edward Whitmont gives a one-page sketch of the four masculine archetypes in *The Symbolic Quest* (Princeton 1969), pp 181–82. Other sources which we have found useful will be mentioned in subsequent notes.

2

THE FEMININE STORIES

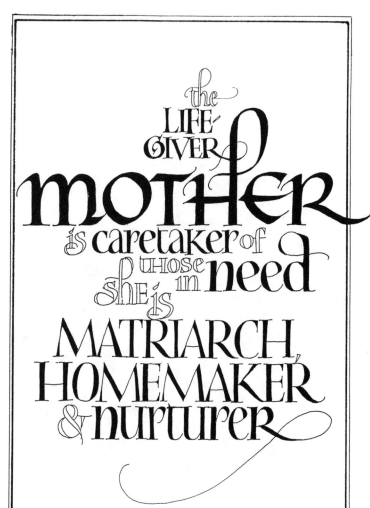

the
LIFE-
GIVER
MOTHER
is caretaker of a
those need
she is
MATRIARCH,
HOMEMAKER
& nurturer

Mother

Mother finds her identity and fulfillment in helping, cherishing, nurturing, and protecting. She is the life-giver. Her natural instinct is to assist all that is in the process of becoming. She sees where other people need assistance or protection, and she goes to their aid. She supports whatever is in need of nurturing and care. Mother encourages others to develop themselves. She is concerned with, and attends to, the comfort and security of those she nourishes. Mother will usually arrange her outer life to include marriage or a nurturing profession, such as social work, teaching or nursing.

Mother is more people-oriented than achievement-oriented and will give of herself, often to the point of exhaustion, when she feels needed by those who rely on her. She is the gracious hostess and the compassionate nurse. She is the patient, uncondescending teacher, and the supportive parent. She finds identity and fulfillment in responding to children, the needy poor, the infirm elderly, the ill, the mentally handicapped, immigrants and disadvantaged minority groups. Patience, sharing, and unselfishness are qualities she values and fosters. She conserves and promotes family values, and is the caretaker of tradition.

Mother feels most useful and comfortable in a relationship where the other is in need—of protection, care, instruction, support, advice, or a good meal. Doing for those in need is more important and fulfilling than relating to a mature peer who has no need of Mother's nurturing qualities. Mother cherishes relationships which have a history, and she is open to new relationships when she sees that they will fit into the family story (for instance, new in-laws, her husband's boss, and other "official" relationships).

If she marries, Mother will be concerned with the career security, social position, and respectability of the father. She will protect and promote whatever enhances his role as father. In fact, she often refers to her husband as "Father" or "Dad" instead of using his first name. Her husband may be mystified to find her suddenly withdrawing support from some hobby of his, or a friendship, or a career choice. Mother is not usually a risk-taker, and she is likely to withdraw support when *her* vision of what is good for the family is threatened. At times, her mate could feel like a provider or an elder son, rather than a husband and companion.

Mother is matriarch and homemaker. How the rooms in the house are used and the way the furniture is selected and arranged usually show her priorities. Often the children will be the focus of the home rather than her husband. What was once a formal dining room is turned into a family room or a playroom for the children, because Mother is more concerned with family togetherness than with creating space for one-on-one adult relating. Mother's children are seen as members of a family before they are experienced as individuals with their own destiny. She places much emphasis on tradition, roles, and shared responsibility, which is based on a child's place in the family.

The dark side of Mother shows itself in indulgent parenting, anxious nursing, smothering mothering, and a distrust of the other's abilities. She might protect and assist when the other person never required it in the first place. She might assist and actively care for the other in order to *feel* useful and needed, not because she *is* needed. She may pass her fears, her prejudices, and even her religious fervors on to those in her care, filling them with a life that is not their own. Mother is not usually preoccupied with goals and achievement. But in mid-life, a frustrated Mother might push her children to achieve and perform in her name. Some bitter Mothers will envy their child's authentic accomplishments.

Mother finds her identity and fulfillment in giving, and she is usually very gracious. She is oriented to giving rather than receiving, and sometimes it is difficult for her to admit when she is in need herself. However, Mother can suddenly become the martyr when she feels she has been taken for granted. She can turn into the injured Queen Bee when she thinks her subjects have not fully appreciated her role in their lives. Mother can become subtly manipulative or quite ruthless when her point of view is not recognized or when she has not received her due. Peer relationships can be difficult for Mother. She is often more impatient with her peers than she is with those who depend on her. Even in casual conversations she tends to instruct or give advice. When she does not feel useful and appreciated, Mother tends to be more exacting than understanding, and more judging than accepting.

Companion

Companion finds her identity and fulfillment in accompanying others, and in being accompanied. She companions others intellectually, spiritually, emotionally, sexually—though not necessarily all four. Her quest is for union with others and with her own self, a union which she accomplishes through a variety of relationships and experiences. For her, the relationship is all, and everything else is subordinate to the relationship, be it with a man or a woman. Her own development requires her to explore individual relationships, because these relationships expose her to new and different experiences. It is in these relationships and experiences that she finds out who she is and who she is not. Like Mother, this is a personal way of relating, but it is individual rather than collective, very much one-on-one. This woman is the devoted companion, intriguing spouse, intense friend, passionate lover, trusted counselor, and inspiring teacher. The Companion values equality, individuality, communication, relatedness.

Companions are usually (at least initially) attentive, adaptable, and accommodating. The expression of the relationship will be in keeping with the interests and needs of the other. However,

COMPANION
devoted companion, intriguing spouse
COMPANION
passionate lover, intense friend, attentive
COMPANION
teacher, devoted companion, intriguing
COMPANION
spouse, passionate lover, intense friend
COMPANION
attentive teacher, devoted companion
COMPANION
intriguing spouse, passionate lover,
COMPANION
intense friend, attentive teacher, devoted
COMPANION
companion, intriguing spouse, passionate
COMPANION

she is never a passive object in a relationship. She promotes the individual interests of her spouse, her children, or her friend, regardless of the consequences for family image or personal security. She is not preoccupied with how her actions appear to others. Traditional roles and the expectations of others do not govern her life or influence her behavior. In or out of a relationship, the Companion's behavior is often considered unconventional. She has a social openness but does not like to get into situations that involve complicated or formal social structures. Social position and financial security, which are a concern for Mother, are quite secondary to the Companion.

A particular function of the Companion is to awaken the individual psyche of the male, and to lead him beyond his role responsibilities toward the formation of a more total personality, often in the second half of life. Her intolerance for roles and for social convention helps a Companion to put a man in touch with his unconscious. Most males need a good Companion at some point in their lives. This is not necessarily the "other woman." Many daughters are Companions to their fathers; some mothers are Companions to their sons; women who are effective spiritual directors for men are often Companions.

It is important to emphasize that the Companion's relationship with a man need not always be sexual. Recall that these women find identity and fulfillment in accompanying intellectually, spiritually, and emotionally. When it is appropriate, there will be sexual expression, but this will not usually take place until a certain depth and psychic union has been reached. For some Companions, this depth might be reached quite quickly.

The Companion is exhilarated by any new relationship and the variety of experiences it promises. If she is artistically or intellectually inclined, she does some of her most creative work when inspired by a relationship. Women who have not thought of themselves as "creative" and find themselves writing poetry when affected by a relationship are often Companions.

Companions can sometimes be quarrelsome and violent. They do not enjoy tension and stormy confrontations, but they often find this way of relating necessary to bring consciousness. They dislike hidden agendas and unconscious thoughts and feelings which disrupt the relationship, and they will use any means possible to improve the relationship and to help the other person to become the best of himself or herself. Although usually diplomatic, a Companion still prefers truth to harmony. A mature Companion is persevering and loyal in her individual relationships and not preoccupied with personal gratification. She is concerned about the welfare of the other and the nature of the relationship, but not to the extent that she neglects her own interests and personal destiny.

To some, the Companion appears to be a very unselfish giver, while to others this very quality makes her look as though she does not have a mind of her own. Irene de Castillejo describes how the tendency only to do things for someone one loves makes it difficult for a Companion to know what she herself really wants.

> She is often accused quite naturally by men of futility or hypocrisy, because when asked what she wants to do, she replies "whatever you like." But it is not hypocrisy. She really means that her desire is to do what he wants. It has not occurred to her to have any special preference. Even if she knew she wanted to dance it would give her no pleasure to do so if her lover was longing to watch a cricket match. This adaptability is not unselfishness and has no particular merit.[1]

The Companion who is a parent sees her children as individuals, with individual personalities and talents, quite apart from their place and roles in the family. She befriends and companions her children, and appreciates them all the more as their personalities unfold. For this reason she is not usually so fascinated by babies as Mother is. In her family, Companion gives more emphasis to individuality and the need for private space, and she is less concerned with togetherness and group activities. The Companion is not inclined to take credit for her children's success, nor will she feel guilty about their failures.

If she does not bring her Companion nature to consciousness, she can turn her young sons into boyfriends and her daughters into girlfriends, by sharing with them information and experiences that are not appropriate to their years. When there is not an adult to companion her, she must be very careful not to let a child fill the void. This is a danger in single-parent homes where the Companion mother is the head of the family. She must be careful not to rob her children of their innocence.

In her professional life the Companion will be more personal than impersonal. She will prefer to relate individually, not collectively as Mother is inclined. A teacher or a social worker who is Companion will accompany rather than instruct or advise. She will be more attentive to the needs of the individual than to the "common good."

The Companion must learn what belongs to a relationship and what does not, what is an appropriate expression of the relationship and what is not. This is where her dark side can show itself. She can put a man in touch with himself, or she can lead him astray. In any relationship, she must learn to let go when the relationship has fulfilled itself, or when it should take another form. If she is between relationships, she must be wary of getting involved simply because she is bored or without direction. She must be careful about turning one form of accompanying into another when it is not appropriate. For instance, a Companion who is mentor might do more harm than good if she lets herself become emotionally involved with the person she is mentoring.

The immature Companion will go from one relationship to another, seeking her own self at the expense of the other. The immature Companion is the flirt and the tease, the lover who is more passionate than compassionate. She is the narcissistic Companion who is so taken up with how she affects others that she forgets about the other in the relationship. She is the self-seeking woman who is compulsive about new experiences, and more interested in the experience than in the person who shares it with her. She is frustrated by those who are not able to offer her the drama of new insights and new experiences. She must learn to be attentive to those whose experience of life differs from her own.

The Companion needs relationships, and she often prefers to accompany or to be accompanied than to do things on her own and for herself. She can all too easily set aside her own interests or activities. As time goes by, she will become resentful as she realizes that she has not developed her own talents, but instead has accompanied others in activities she did not necessarily enjoy. This dependent Companion will probably make unrealistic demands on another for time and attention. The Companion must learn to accompany her own self, not just others.

Mother and Companion are attuned to and influenced by the needs of other people. The difference between them is this: Mother finds her identity and fulfillment in doing *for others*. Companion finds hers in doing *with the Other*.

Amazon

The Amazon is the self-contained woman who finds her identity and fulfillment in managing the outer world. She is instinctively drawn toward outward achievements. She sets her own goals and participates in the activities of her choice with clear focus. The Amazon is a zealous woman with a particular inborn energy and drive. She strives not only to succeed but to excel in her field of endeavor. She is energized by competition and achievement. Independence, excellence, and power are driving forces in her life.

The Amazon is more concerned with collective and impersonal values than she is with people and relationships. She finds identity in planning, organizing, competing, and succeeding. Order and efficiency are qualities she values. The Amazon feels fulfilled when she is in control of the situation. If she has strong moral values, she uses her gifts with integrity. She may also be a schemer, reaching her goal through questionable methods.

The Amazon is the woman in politics, and the determined actress who wants to make a name for herself. She is the sportswoman, and the woman who is active in the business world. She is the confident teacher who takes pride in passing on knowledge. She is often a successful entrepreneur, or a decorated member of the military. The extraverted Amazon is usually visible and identifiable, but by no means is every Amazon forceful or vocal. She is also the reserved Mother Superior who guides her congregation wisely. Nor is her job always prestigious or high-profile. She is the quiet secretary who takes pride in seeing that the office runs smoothly, and the loyal worker who is indispensable on the assembly line. She is the teacher who instructs with clarity and purpose, conveying tangible truths.

Not all Amazons work outside the home. Some are housekeepers who stay at home to manage the household. But after a period of time, many Amazons no longer feel sufficiently taken up by their home or their personal relationships, and so they turn to a task outside the home.

Artists and writers who are Amazons bring to their work many of the qualities that flow from their archetype. Their themes are independence, achievement, power, and the strength of the

The
Amazon
is the self-
contained
woman who
finds her identity
et fulfillment in
managing the outer
world. She is instinct-
ively drawn toward out-
ward achievements. She
sets her own goals et participates in activities of her choice

Amazon

g. stevens

tient and attentive to what is undeveloped in herself and others. A wise woman, and often a courageous woman, she knows when to act and when to refrain from acting. She does not act for the sake of activity, nor does she compete for the sake of competition. A mature Amazon is not preoccupied with achieving to such an extent that she neglects her own values and feelings. She is also attentive to the values and feelings of others, and does not view them as awkward complications. However independent and capable she may be, the discerning Amazon never fails to recognize that there is legitimate authority and wisdom outside herself.

In her relationships with men, the Amazon can be the refreshing companion who makes no demands. She and the male act as mutual challengers. Her own development does not depend on the male's response unless she lets it. Independence is the Amazon's watchword, professionally and in her personal relationships. If she marries, she often thinks of the marriage as an "accomplishment" or a "partnership."

The Amazon who is a parent is inclined to see her children in the light of their potential and their ability to achieve. She will put emphasis on goals—on getting and doing, rather than on being and learning. Her children may not feel valued for their own sakes. An Amazon parent whose ambition and energies exceed the needs of the home can become an impatient mother and a demanding housekeeper. She can go to such extremes as to wake her children at three o'clock in the morning to rearrange their closets. A demanding perfectionist, she will scrub clean floors and dust dustless furniture. This is the Amazon who *needs* activities outside the home, because her fulltime presence in the home eventually hinders a good relationship with her children. She will be a happier woman, a better parent and wife, when she is not identified totally with the home.

The Amazon is a determined woman who is exacting of others. Often, unaware of her own limitations, she dwells on the faults and failures of others. A perfectionist, she insists that if you want a job done well you have to do it yourself. She may not appreciate the effort of others, and in the name of perfection and efficiency she might take over a project or activity that rightly belongs to another. The immature Amazon is a difficult person to work for, and an impossible person to work with. Another dark side of the Amazon shows itself when she manipulates others into working on a project that enhances her own reputation. Sometimes she claims another's effort as her own, and does not give credit where credit is due.

Mediatrix

The Mediatrix or "mediumistic woman" has access to the collective unconscious and finds her identity and fulfillment in mediating the world of the unconscious.[2] She is permeated by the non-tangible atmosphere of her surroundings and the latent spirit of her time. She is the receptive container for a flow of information that originates outside herself, and she helps others to "see" what is invisible. She senses what is going on under the surface of a group or an event and is drawn to express it. The Mediatrix has an uncanny sensitivity to the conscious and unconscious psychological needs of other people. This woman is rarely a public person in her role as Mediatrix, but sometimes she does find a place to exercise her particular gift in arts and skills that society considers more or less esoteric—such as painting, creative writing, contemplation, counseling, astrology, graphology, herbal medicine, and some forms of ministry. (Not all women involved in these activities are mediumistic women.)

The Mediatrix often feels as though she lives in two different worlds at the same time. She is connected to the living, the ordinary, the personal—and at the same time to the non-living, the supernatural, and the universal. She is attuned to a larger reality and is therefore influenced by a particular kind of "knowing."

Often the Mediatrix is affected by the unconscious of another person, even someone whom she does not know well, and she will sometimes dream on behalf of this person.

The Mediatrix is the reverent woman who symbolizes and ritualizes through worship and art. She does this for herself and for others. She can often feel apart and "different" from others. She is usually an unconventional person, but she is not preoccupied with her self-image or with how other people perceive her. Her main concern is her role as interpreter. Personal power and financial security are not of great importance. Goals do not motivate her, and competition exhausts her.

The Mediatrix is caught in a tension between two kinds of reality: she must live a conventional life in the tangible world and at the same time dwell in the larger non-tangible world of symbols and "knowing." It takes a long time before a Mediatrix can peacefully live with integrity in both worlds, denying neither one.

The Mediatrix has an important role in mediating the world of the unconscious to men. She often finds herself assisting other people in dying, especially men. In some cases she might be aware of what she is doing, but often enough her role is unplanned and unconscious. Irene de Castillejo describes this facet of the Mediatrix. On one occasion she visited a man in hospital whom she knew only casually. Later she visited him in his home.

> To my surprise he told me intimate things of his life which he had never before mentioned to anyone. I said almost nothing but when I rose to leave I kissed him lightly on the forehead. To my bewilderment he burst into tears. Without knowing at all what I was doing I had freed him from the dry prison of his intellect in which he had been immured and put him in touch with his own unconscious feeling, with its promise for the future. Next day his wife told me I was the only person he wanted to see. I sat by his bed and listened to his delirium. But it was no longer guilt-ridden. He had already embarked on a journey. He died that night.[3]

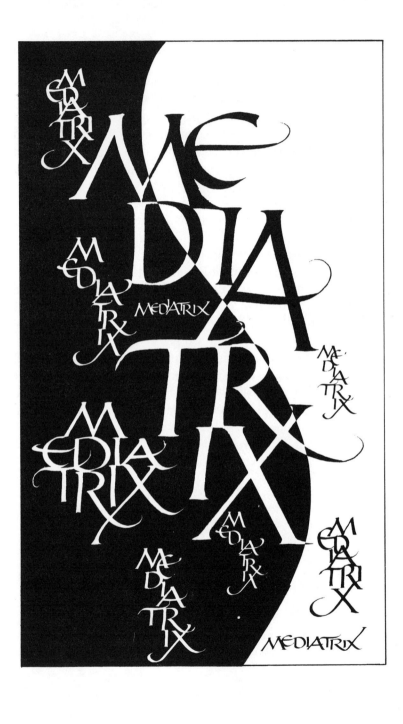

The Mediatrix will sometimes transmit knowledge prematurely, without even realizing that she is doing this. As a parent she must be careful that her insights from the unconscious do not spill over onto her children, frustrating their need to learn for themselves.

The immature mediumistic woman appears unfocused and vague. Initially she is confused, not knowing what thoughts and feelings are her own and what is coming to her from the unconscious. She must develop a strong ego so that she can differentiate the thoughts and feelings that come to her. This is more difficult for the Mediatrix than for other women. If she does not mature in wisdom and discernment, she will become very tormented, disruptive both to herself and to others. Often the Mediatrix needs the understanding and love of a strong individual, or the loyalty of a particular group, to help her to overcome the inner confusion and the self-doubts that come with her ability to "know." In the process of becoming more directed, she must be careful not to subsume elements of her own personality in the personality of the man she loves. Often the Mediatrix doesn't know if she is expressing her own needs or those of the person she cares for. She doesn't know if she is expressing her own interests or those of the group that supports her.

The dark side of the Mediatrix shows itself most often in inflated thoughts and actions. Many artists and writers who are mediumistic overestimate their message and abilities, and think that their work is above sound critique. When negative comments come their way they become arrogant or feel victimized. Some contemplative women use reflection and meditation as an escape from the mundane and the ordinary, setting themselves apart from others. Subtly seductive women will exaggerate their abilities in order to intrigue and mystify those who are fascinated by the unknown. The most vicious of all is the Mediatrix who distorts and misinterperts the contents of the unconscious in order to have power over people and situations.

Notes

1. Guild of Pastoral Psychology, Guild Lecture #115, London 1961.
2. "Collective unconscious" is Jung's term for the level of reality where individual consciousness disappears and all of humankind is fused into one common humanity. The collective unconscious helps to explain why people of every era, ancient and modern, from Polynesia to Iceland, tend to produce the same archetypal images and symbols.
3. Irene Claremont de Castillejo, *Knowing Woman* (Harper & Row, 1973), p 68.

3

THE MASCULINE STORIES

loving · providing and protecting ·

Father

· an image of God · always present ·

Father

Father finds his identity and fulfillment in providing and protecting. He is a natural complement to Mother and shares many of her nurturing qualities. Whether he is married or not, and whether he is a parent or not, Father enjoys those roles where he can provide for others and protect their well-being. His priority is the welfare of his brood, whatever that might be—his family, his employees, his pupils, his patients, his parish, whoever is in his care. He likes to direct things in a protective way, and he usually enjoys the leadership roles that fall to him in his household and outside it. Father is not concerned with power for its own sake. He is simply preoccupied with looking after the welfare of those in his care, and protecting them against whatever may threaten their well-being.

Father is the hospitable host who tends to the needs of his guests. He takes pleasure in seeing his family assembled, whether it be in church on Sunday, or on a ski trip with his children, or at the picnic he plans for his employees.

The Judeo-Christian image of God as Father comes from the bright side of this archetype. Jesus used this image to express the idea of God as a faithful lover who is always present to his people, caring and providing for them. This is the Father at his best.

Father is strict in the performance of what he considers his duty, and he expects the same sense of discipline from others. He gives orders and he expects them to be obeyed. He is not necessarily stern or authoritarian, because he may have learned the qualities of gentleness and benevolence. His word may not always sound like law—but his word is usually directive. He is not necessarily a perfectionist who demands perfection of others, but one always senses that his way is the better way of doing things. Even a gentle Father gives the impression that there is no room for discussion once he has come to a conclusion. Because he takes pride

31

in providing for others, he likes to be asked for help. But he is reluctant to ask others for help in turn.

He enjoys taking responsibility, and his main concern for his own children is that they will be prepared for having responsibility. In accomplishing this role, he often sets his children free from home and mother, and he facilitates their transition into the wider world. He fosters in his children the development of whatever skills they most need to deal effectively with the world at large. He will not always be supportive of hobbies which seem aimless to him, or of activities which do not build character for adult life. He will worry over the child who cannot seem to find direction in life as quickly as he himself did.

Father is the guardian of tradition and convention. His values tend to be those that he himself was taught as a child, and he considers as his duty whatever was so considered by those in authority over him. He values stability and permanence, the status quo, and he wants to pass on to his children whatever values have worked for him. These are usually the collective values of his own father's era, and the prevailing values of society at large. Many public leaders, from Presidents to Popes, are Fathers who owe their popularity to their emphasis on traditional values and conventional morality. For Father, the right way to do things is the way they have "always been done."

Father is conservative in the best sense, and at his best he produces stability. But he does so at a price. He holds as his own the collective values of the past, and he wants to hand on these values to those in his care. But he is not always reflective or discriminating about individual items in that collective package. The blind spots in the prevailing social system tend to be his own blind spots. Father tends to be threatened by criticism of the status quo, in his own family and in society. He does not usually encourage independent thinking or new ways of looking at things, especially from people who rely on his care. What other people might consider a "creative" or "original" idea, Father tends to see as disruptive, or even immoral and destructive. If things are outside his control and changing all around him, he is determined at least to keep up appearances, as ordained by public opinion.[1]

Father tends to relate to other people insofar as they rely on his care, and so he knows others as children or subjects. He has difficulty relating to others as true peers, individuals in their own right, one-on-one. His social life might be confined to "official" relationships—such as with relatives, in-laws, employees, clients, patients, parishioners—where he can conduct the relationship out of his role as Father, on "official" grounds. Father needs to become a full and authentic participant *in* the life of his family, not just a guardian *over* his brood. Genuine participation gives him a chance to relate to others as peers, and this will protect him from becoming authoritarian and condescending in his dealings with others.

If Father is a natural leader, he can also be a dictator and a tyrant. This is not to suggest that he considers his own authority to be ultimate. Often enough, Fathers who are rigid and authoritarian need to submit themselves to an authority greater than themselves, such as a political or religious leader, or someone in whom they find their own values embodied. Thus, a Father who demands unquestioning obedience from his subordinates often gives the same unquestioning obedience to his own superiors. This dynamic leads finally to fascism, which is the ultimate social expression of Father-dominance.[2] Father must learn to be discriminating about the collective values which take hold of him. Otherwise his own leadership will come across as rigid and one-sided, cold and inflexible.

Father and Mother are natural complements to each other. They tend to look for and find each other when it comes time to marry and raise a family. They often call each other "Father" and "Mother" long after their children have left home. In the second half of life, both Mother and Father need to explore another dimension of their archetype or a second archetype—especially when they do not have grandchildren or other young people around them whom they can mother and father in their special way.

Seeker

The Seeker finds his identity and fulfillment precisely in the search for identity and fulfillment. This might seem like a circular way of defining the Seeker, but it highlights the fact that open-ended searching and questing are a way of life for him in anything he does, and in whatever role he finds himself. While Father knows his identity insofar as he is connected *with* collective and traditional values, the Seeker is always trying to differentiate himself *from* the expectations and conventions that surround him. He wants above all to discover his own individuality—who he is in himself—and this is a quest that never tires him.

The Seeker is interested in peer relationships with a whole variety of men and women. He is personable, he makes a good first impression, and people usually like him before they know much about him. The Seeker is usually open to any kind of companionship, because he discovers who he is by relating to different people in a variety of situations. Father knows he is Father, and his identity is readily accessible to him. Not so the Seeker, who needs the mirror of his relationships with other men and women in order to find out what he himself is all about.

The Seeker "does his own thing" more than any other archetype. He is always off on new adventures. Understand "adventures" in a metaphorical sense. The Seeker might never leave home or set off in new geographical directions. He might stay right at home, doing his own thing in his own territory. But he is always off into new projects, new hobbies, new ideas, and the attractions of new relationships.

At his best, the Seeker has much to offer. He is open-minded, and he easily assimilates new ways of doing things. In fact, he is usually looking for a better way. He is enthusiastic about activities that interest him, and he often brings a refreshing point of view to an enterprise. He can be a man of high ideals who satisfies his thirst for adventure through missionary work in a foreign land, or as a Peace Corps volunteer. He is the explorer and the tour guide. He is the photographer who uses a camera to capture his perception of the world.

Seekers tend to shy away from large and complex organizations. They are often found running a small business, or plying a trade where they can be their own boss. Frequently their recreational interests develop into a business occupation. By no means are all Seekers self-employed. They also hold responsible positions in large organizations. When they work for others, Seekers often put as much time into their off-hours activities and hobbies as they do into their job.

The Seeker is not always ready to put serious effort into his open-endedness and make it productive. He has difficulty finding the job that is right for him, and he is put off by jobs that he thinks are beneath him or too confining for him. He wants a career because people expect it of him. But he is not always ready to invest his energy in any single career, because this might shackle his searching. The mature Seeker is able to settle into a job that fits his interests. But he usually has an eye open for a new opportunity, and he is capable of risking his financial security and that of his family for the sake of a venture that grabs his interest.

The Seeker often acts as though the rules don't apply to him. The fact is that he has his own set of rules, most of which have to do with protecting his freedom and his integrity as a Seeker. He inevitably comes into conflict with Father and Mother, who have commitments to tradition and convention, stability and permanence. The immature Seeker does not appreciate any such values, which put restraints on his independence. This is where the Seeker shows his dark side, which consists in full-fledged irre-

Seeker

finds his identity
and fulfillment
in the search
for identity
and fulfillment.

sponsibility. One of the classical names for this archetype is "Eternal Boy," a good image for describing the immature Seeker. Another image is found in the title of Dan Kiley's bestseller, *The Peter Pan Syndrome*. Peter Pan is the Eternal Boy, the Seeker who never grows up.

In their personal relationships, the Seeker and his feminine counterpart the Companion have some traits in common. Both are inclined to "love 'em and leave 'em." The Companion is usually better at loving, the Seeker at leaving.[3] He might not be sexually promiscuous, but he tends to be fickle in his friendships. When a relationship gets stormy, he is inclined to walk away from it rather than deal with it thoroughly. As a result, his life is often filled with loneliness. He looks for friends, he needs to belong somewhere, and the more he looks the more lonely he feels. Eternal Boys are searching for a Never Never Land which eventually turns into a prison for them. "In this prison they are ravaged by loneliness but pretend to have friends; they are trapped in self-doubt but pretend to be confident . . . Worst of all, they are consumed by isolation and pretend they are loved."[4]

If he does not learn self-discipline, the Seeker will lack stability and never find for himself the personal identity for which he is always seeking. He will lack stability to the point of being totally undependable, a poor provider in his family, an undependable partner in business. He is likely to have a whole gamut of interesting acquaintances, but few enduring friendships. His narcissism keeps him focused on what he can get out of a relationship, and he will not make much effort to bring anything to it. The Seeker who never grows up is inclined to blame others for his failures, refusing to acknowledge that he has brought his own misfortunes on himself. He set out to be unique and doesn't realize that he has become a stereotype of the Eternal Boy.

Warrior

Warrior finds his identity and fulfillment in accomplishing in the outer world. He is the go-getter who sets goals for himself and gets things done. His energy is directed toward accomplishing the task, winning the game, executing the plan, conquering the territory, seizing the prize. He is a good competitor who is not afraid of a struggle or fight. In fact he thrives on competition, which often brings out the best of his talents. His efficiency is not seriously affected by disharmony or tensions among the people around him, because his energy is directed more toward the task and the goal than toward people. As a result, he can often keep a cool head in the midst of stressful situations.

The Warrior archetype is especially useful as a man is establishing a place for himself in society, in a business or in a profession. This is *the* socially approved archetype for a man in his twenties or thirties. A man of that age who is not a Warrior and who is not psychically energized by the Warrior story often finds himself at odds with what the world, and perhaps his own family, wants from him. This is not to suggest that all Warriors are committed to existing structures and the status quo. If they are motivated by a vision of new and better things, Warriors can be revolutionaries in their field. In any realm, the Warrior's natural drive to accomplish his goal can contribute significant benefits to society. This can include the field of international relations: many Warriors are pacifists.

The Warrior likes to manage power. This is a satisfying end in itself, and he is often very good at it. The Warrior always has a keen sense of where the power lies in any organization, and he knows how to work within the power structure in order to accomplish his own goals. He is attentive to the hierarchy of power, and he finds satisfaction in the ranks, titles, and perquisites that come with a position. The titles and "perks" are often as important to him as the money he makes.

The Warrior is energized by whatever is doable, and it is enough for him that a given task *is* doable. He often finds it difficult to be receptive to ideas and values that are bigger than the project or struggle at hand. He has to develop strong personal values which will make him ask whether the doable task is *worth* doing, and how it affects others. He has to acquire a wisdom which reaches beyond the moment of this task, and he must learn to appreciate the wisdom and personal values of others. Otherwise he will be concerned only with what can be accomplished, and he can turn out to be a cutthroat in his field. The world has profited much from the focused energies of Warriors who get things done efficiently. It has also suffered at the hands of Warriors who act only in the service of achieving their own goals. Warriors must be careful not to adopt the research and ideas of others, claiming them as their own for power or profit.

Warriors are more concerned with efficiency than with people. If they are in executive positions, they need to seek advice about the dynamics of human relationships and become sensitive to their "human resources" (an interesting term, reflecting the Warrior's focus on the collective and the impersonal). The persons who are best equipped to make staffing decisions, and who have their finger on the people-pulse of the organization, are not usually Warriors themselves. The executive Warrior has to learn to consult qualified people who possess a wisdom that is different from his own. But such consultation is difficult for him. When push comes to shove, the Warrior is more inclined to save the enterprise than to look after the welfare of the people involved.

Dealing with people and their interests is one of the Warrior's more difficult jobs. Warriors in positions of leadership often speak of their "human resources" as if they were pieces on a chess board. This reflects the fact that, for the Warrior, people and relation-

WARRIOR

ships tend to be secondary to the task at hand. The Warrior can of course learn the skills of dealing with people. But he has to be careful not to use this knowledge in a Warrior-like fashion, by treating people as objects to be manipulated in the service of his goal. Many popular books and programs which promise wealth and success foster the concept of learning how to manipulate other people (and the authors of these programs prove their point and accomplish their own goals with each sale). Warriors have to be careful about how their natural drives, useful in business, flow into their personal lives. Warriors are intent on conquering, and the immature Warrior deals with other people as conquests to be won. This can be especially true of his relationships with women.

The Warrior is easily recognizable in the world of big business and large institutions, but these are not his only arenas. Most professional athletes are Warriors, as are the soldiers of fortune in any era. A Warrior might also be a counselor, a teacher, a pastor, a doctor, or a social worker.

Warriors in the helping professions need to become sensitive to the kind of power they exercise over other people. The Warrior's gift for managing power can degenerate into a drive to have control over others. This drive might be unconscious and unfocused in the Warrior's own mind, but it is very dangerous, especially in the helping professions, because people in need of help freely hand over power and control to their helper. A doctor or pastor or counselor who is a Warrior needs to work hard at developing empathy with his clients, and he must understand his own tendency to want success in dealing with their problems. Otherwise he will misuse the power he has to help them. Instead of freeing them, he will bind them to himself. Instead of helping them, he will subtly use his patients or clients to enrich his bank account and to enhance his own name and professional reputation.

In the first part of his life, the Warrior's goals are usually tangible, measurable accomplishments related to success or prosperity or status in his field of endeavor. In the second half of life these "outer" values tend to fade in importance. The mature Warrior starts to transcend beyond accomplishments, and he begins directing his energies toward "inner" goals like achieving true wisdom. For the Warrior, wisdom consists above all in the ability to see the connections among all of life's pursuits and values. The wise Warrior is one who has learned to keep in mind the good of others and the good of the whole. If he does not enlarge his own inner world and acquire a larger view of the outer world, the Warrior's life will be marked by *excess*. He will be willful and determined and task-oriented at the expense of all other life-giving values.

Sage

The Sage finds his identity and fulfillment in drawing forth meaning for himself and for others. While the Warrior is oriented to the outer world, the Sage is drawn toward the inner world of meaning. He organizes his world around a philosophy, a system of significance, a search for meaning. His inner drive is to put himself and others in touch with reason, mind, thought, spirit, or whatever name he might give to ideas worth considering simply because they are worthwhile ideas. The Sage is found not only in the professions of teaching and scholarship. He might be a cabinet-maker, a mechanic or a gardener, a "cracker-barrel philosopher."

The Sage sees the world against the background of his personal theories, the mental models he has constructed for understanding the world and his own experience. The Sage does not know how to deal effectively with the things that happen around him until he can fit them into one of his mental models. New data and new facts are gradually worked into his personal philosophy, which is usually "in motion" because the Sage is always revising his system of significance. What he most likes to do, even in the midst of a busy agenda, is ponder over the meaning of things. For the Sage, meaning takes precedence over doing.

The Sage is idea-oriented rather than people-oriented. He might be a good people-person, but his best contact with other people takes place through sharing ideas and theories and visions. He is not usually good at small talk, which is an effort for him. At social events the Sage likes to get into discussions over ideas and theories. For him, these are stimulating conversations; others might hear them as arguments.

At his best, the Sage is a prophet. Like most prophets, he often feels that he is on the margins of the groups or organizations to which he belongs. This happens because the Sage does not usually hold as his own the existing collective values of society. Even when he does not set out to be critical or argumentative, his observations often turn out to be threatening to people who hold more conventional views. When he feels marginal, the Sage finds grounding and comfort in the fact that when he is at his best, he does help others to enlarge their vision and see a broader picture.

The Sage who has a professional education is often on the cutting edge of new developments in his field. But competition does not excite him or motivate him, and this is where he is quite opposite to the Warrior. The Sage tends to back off from highly competitive situations because he knows they will drain his energy rather than stimulate him. He is energized by playing with ideas, honing them until they fit into an over-all theory. The Sage does not usually like to go into action until he can see the larger picture. When he wants to implement his ideas in the outer world, he sometimes discovers that he is not the man who has the practical know-how or the contacts for getting things done. Sages know whose judgment they trust, but the people in whom they have the most confidence are not necessarily the right people to

finds identity and
fulfillment in drawing
forth meaning for
himself and for others.

know when it comes to implementing an idea. The Sage can also lack patience for dealing with practical detail, and with processes that involve bringing people along with his ideas.

One of the dark sides of the Sage is that he never gets anything done. He can't translate his ideas into realities, and so he finds himself at odds with the outer world that is so distant from his theoretical visions. The "absent-minded professor" is a stereotype of this dark side of the Sage, especially the introverted type.

Moreover, the Sage is not necessarily "wise." Any man, any woman acquires true wisdom only through time and experience and serious reflection. There are wise men and women found among all the archetypes, and true wisdom is not restricted to the Sage. "Wise Man" happens to be one of the classical mythical names for this archetype—but this figure also appears in literature as Sorcerer or Charlatan.

The Sage is convinced that there is a meaning to be found in anything that happens, and he can easily put his personal world-view in front of facts and events that contradict him. The immature Sage has an inflated view of his own theories. He takes criticism of his ideas as a personal attack on himself, and he is jealous of the contributions of others. The insecure Sage dismisses a new idea from another source with "I've thought of that— What's so original?" Maybe he has had similar thoughts, but he never took the time to explore them thoroughly. Or he was unwilling to risk public critique of his own ideas. The immature Sage pretends at wisdom which he does not really possess, and deludes himself into believing his own pretensions. Then he is likely to become the kind of fool that Shakespeare gave us in Polonius, who is not considered wise by anyone but himself.

The Sage's forte is the world of conscious meaning. This is where he is quite different from his feminine counterpart, the Mediatrix, who mediates the world of *un*conscious meaning. The Sage needs to learn the positive qualities of the Mediatrix, especially when he is tempted to link anything and everything into theories which only take reason and rationality into account. Sages stand at the center of development and progress in any field; they bring about expansion of the frontiers of knowledge. The educated Sage is usually knowledgeable—but again, he is not always wise. True wisdom involves an awareness of how everything belongs to a whole. This is a "diffuse" awareness which the Sage (and any man) needs as a complement to his "focused" consciousness.[5]

The domain of diffuse awareness is often called a man's "inner feminine." Among the four masculine archetypes, the Sage is the man who is most inclined to get in touch with his inner feminine. But this usually requires an effort, particularly for the Sage who dedicates himself to analytic and scientific disciplines which place so much emphasis on reason and rationality. The Sage must open himself to the unconscious, and become attentive to his hunches and dreams and inarticulate thoughts and feelings. He will then enlarge his philosophy to include a healthy sense of the non-rational, the mysterious, and all the rich dimensions of life which forever elude sharp focus. For many Sages, this is the task of the second half of life.

Notes

1. Murray Stein, "The Devouring Father," in *Fathers and Mothers* (Spring Publications, 1973), pp 64–74.
2. Anthony Stevens, *Archetypes* (Quill, 1983), pp 132–33.
3. Edward Whitmont, *The Symbolic Quest* (Princeton, 1969), p 182.
4. Dan Kiley, *The Peter Pan Syndrome* (Avon, 1983), p 38.
5. The helpful terms "diffuse awareness" and "focused consciousness," which we will use again in Chapter 9, come from Irene de Castillejo, *Knowing Woman* (Harper & Row, 1973), pp 73–89.

4

NAMING YOUR STORY

After hearing the Great Stories, a woman in her mid-twenties said "I think I identify with all of the feminine stories, and I can't tell which one is mine." A man of about the same age crossed the boundaries of masculine and feminine when he said "I'm not gay, but the story of the Companion says more about me than any of the masculine archetypes."

Reactions like these are quite common, right after people have heard the stories and before they have had a chance to reflect on them. Age has something to do with this reaction. Many men and women under thirty are still exploring their identity, and they aren't yet sure about the Great Story they can call their own. A young man or woman can be living one or another of the archetypes in a very clear and recognizable way. Their close friends might recognize the archetype, but they can't name it for themselves. This is normal enough. It takes many of us time and reflection to be able to name *for ourselves* what other people often pick up from us the first time they meet us.

Young or old, everyone can find something of themselves in all of the Great Stories. The mature person has touched base with many of the activities described in all eight of the stories. But we don't find *identity and fulfillment* in all of the stories. These key words appear at the beginning of each description, and we now have to see what they imply.

```
            MOTHER                        FATHER
AMAZON———————MEDIATRIX      WARRIOR———————SAGE
           COMPANION                      SEEKER
```

This diagram shows how each archetype has an *opposite* archetype. For example, Mother and Companion are opposite ways of relating to other people. Mother relates to people in a collective way, the Companion in an individual way. This does not mean that Mother is incapable of companioning another person, or that the Companion is not good at mothering. But Mother will companion in a motherly way, and in any relationship she will habitually exhibit the qualities of Mother described in Chapter 2. The Companion on the other hand will nurture her children as any good parent does, but her style of parenting will be quite different from Mother's. In her parenting, she will habitually exhibit the qualities of the Companion.

The same is true for Father and Seeker. Father can be open-minded and adventuresome (prime qualities of the Seeker), just as the Seeker can concern himself with providing well for his family (a prime quality of Father). In speaking of "opposite" archetypes, therefore, we are not suggesting that people act *constantly* or *only* according to their favored archetypes. What the eight great stories try to illustrate is our *habitual* way of being in the world. To use again the example of parenting, Father and Seeker will have different styles and will habitually—but not constantly—exhibit the qualities of their archetype in their parenting.

Amazon and Mediatrix are opposite ways of relating to the non-personal world, or that portion of a woman's life which is not focused on personal relationships. The same is true for Warrior and Sage. Again, we are not suggesting that Mediatrix and Sage are unable or unwilling to accomplish in the outer world. Many of them are very accomplished, but for them accomplishment has a different priority than it has for the Amazon and Warrior. The priority of the Sage and Mediatrix is to mediate meaning in their special ways. If they accomplish in the outer world, they see their accomplishment as a happy by-product of their main interest, which is to mediate meaning. Conversely, the Amazon and Warrior are perfectly capable of dealing with the world of thought and spirit. But their main priority is to *accomplish* something with their ideas. Growing in wisdom is not usually a goal in itself but rather a fruit of their involvement in worthwhile projects and tasks.

The same thing applies to Amazon and Mediatrix, Warrior and Sage, as we said above: The archetypes illustrate our habitual—but not constant—way of being in the world and going about things. The next two chapters will give ample illustrations of the different "styles" that each archetype exhibits in activities that are familiar to all of us, such as parenting or pursuing a career.

At some time in our lives, or even throughout our lives, most of us get involved in the activities belonging to Great Stories other than our own. For example, the Seeker has to learn how to be responsible and how to manage his household. In other words, he has to do more in life than be a Seeker, doing the Seeker's thing. The Amazon has to learn how to love and be intimate, how to be open to the unseen and the unconscious. She has to do more in life than be an Amazon, doing the Amazon's thing.

The Sage who only does the Sage's thing will never get his ideas out there and translate them into action. He has to learn some of the ways of the Warrior. Otherwise the mental models through which he sees life will become more and more removed from the real world where people live. The Mediatrix who only does the Mediatrix's thing will be vague and unfocused, and she will not develop confidence in herself. Her gifts and her message will never benefit other people unless she learns how to do for herself some of what the Amazon does.

Men and women who refuse to participate in any story but their own are usually stereotypes of their archetype. Like Archie Bunker, they have their colorful and amusing side. They might be interesting "characters" to people who know them casually, but it is a different experience if you have to live with them. To anyone who really knows them they are narrow-minded and odd.

These examples show how people can and must identify *with*

certain portions of all the Great Stories. But at the same time, none of us finds our personal identity and fulfillment *in* all of the stories.

Upon hearing the Great Stories, some people quickly identify their archetype, recognizing it as the story they have lived ever since they were little. If you are not one of these people, here is a process of reflection you can use to identify your archetype:

1. Read chapter 2 or chapter 3 again. Read the chapter that belongs to your gender, male or female. Don't be bothered at this point with the ways you might identify with qualities of the opposite sex; for now, stay with the chapter that describes the archetypes of your gender. Read the descriptions slowly.
2. Read the descriptions a second time *aloud* to yourself.
3. Among all of the activities described in the four Great Stories that pertain to my gender, which activities give me the most joy, the most satisfaction? Where do I feel most comfortable? If I were able to spend my time however I wanted, given my talents and interests, which of the stories best describes what I would be doing?
4. In which of the stories do I most feel *me?* In which of these stories am I the most *myself?* Which is the story that best explains the rhythm of my life and the choices I have made?
5. Which of the activities described in the Great Stories drain me the most? What activities frustrate me? Which of the stories describes how I *least* prefer to spend my time and energy? Which story sounds very foreign to me? Your dominant story is usually the one that is *opposite* to the story that least appeals to you.
6. Have a friend who knows you well read the Great Stories, and ask your friend to name your story. People who know us well can often name our archetype more easily than we can name it for ourselves.

At this point, after you have done a bit of reflection, you might still find yourself wavering between a couple of archetypes. In fact, many people find identity and fulfillment in *two* of the Great Stories. We will now go on to explain why.

In the diagram, the archetypes that are printed vertically (Mother and Companion, Father and Seeker) have to do with our ways of relating to other people. The archetypes that lie on the horizontal (Amazon and Mediatrix, Warrior and Sage) have to do with the non-personal dimension of life: the outer world, the world of ideas, and the realm of the unconscious. Two different dimensions of life, two different planes of activity, the personal and the non-personal. So it is not surprising that many people identify with *two* archetypes, one for the personal world and one for the impersonal world.

As you answered the questions we gave above, you might have found that you related strongly to two of the archetypes, so that you find yourself along one of the diagonal planes indicated in the diagram. For example, a man might be Father-Warrior, or Father-Sage, or Seeker-Sage, or Seeker-Warrior. Similarly with the feminine archetypes. A woman might be Mother-Amazon, or Amazon-Companion, and so on. (No one finds identity and fulfillment in the archetype *opposite* to his or her dominant archetype, for reasons that we will make clear as we go on.)

Some people find total satisfaction throughout their lives in just one archetype, and as their lives unfold they develop different facets of this story. This is especially true of Mother and Father. When their own children grow up and leave home, they bring their qualities of nurturing and providing to other tasks and activities. Mother, for example, might continue mothering through a profession like teaching or nursing or social work. Father might already have ample opportunities for living out his story in his profession or business, where he finds fulfillment in leading, caring, and providing for others.

But most people find their identity in *two* of the Great Stories. In this case, one story is usually the dominant force in a person's life, and the other is a kind of "auxiliary" story. The Mediatrix, for instance, does not easily find a role or a profession in which she can consistently exercise her mediumistic qualities. So while she finds her *identity* in this archetype, she often lacks opportunities to find much *fulfillment* in it. The Mediatrix invariably needs a second archetype—Mother or Companion—which will help her to connect with people, and to develop a stable ego and a good self-image.

The Seeker, with all of his love for new adventures and new relationships, invariably needs a second archetype to help him develop stability and a sense of responsibility. The Warrior or the Sage archetype will function as his "auxiliary" story and enable him to connect with a world that is more solid and objective than his Seeker-world of dreams and limitless opportunities. The Seeker's auxiliary archetype—Warrior or Sage—is often what enables him to grow up and accept responsibility. To put it the other way around, the Seeker without an auxiliary story is likely to remain an Eternal Boy who never settles down or accomplishes anything in life.

The man who is Warrior and the woman who is Amazon are also enriched by a second archetype. Their inner drive toward success and accomplishing their goals can result in a certain harshness and insensitivity to the needs of other people. Warriors and Amazons without an auxiliary archetype lack warmth and have a "steel-edged" quality about them. Their auxiliary story (Father or Seeker, Mother or Companion) enables the Warrior and Amazon to step back from their work, to connect with their humanness, and to relate to other people in a way that is not task-oriented.

All of these examples show how, for many people, a second archetype is needed for a balance in life.

We don't necessarily develop two of the Great Stories at once. For many people, a second or auxiliary archetype emerges only in the second half of life. To give a very common example, a Mother who has found identity and fulfillment in raising children during the first half of her life might get interested in public life, run for a political office, or set up a business in the second half of life. Her second archetype is the Amazon, and it emerges only later in her life. To flip this example the other way around, an Amazon might manage her marriage and her children very successfully in the first half of life. Amazon is her dominant archetype, parenting is her task, and she approaches it in her Amazon way. In the second half of life, she might be drawn to the Mother archetype, awakening to it for the first time in her life. She might take up a nurturing profession outside the home; and within the family, she might turn out to be more "motherly" to her grandchildren than she ever was to her own children.

Part of the challenge of the midlife transition is the call to enter into another of the Great Stories. For some people, the challenge is frightening and confusing, and in that case the midlife transition becomes the "midlife crisis" that we hear so much about. How this can happen is easy enough to understand. We have found identity and fulfillment in one archetype, we have been satisfied by it and have become comfortable in it—and suddenly we start waking up in the morning with no energy for the things that used to motivate and nourish us.

The next chapters will talk more about the problems of midlife and the shift in archetypes that tends to take place at that time. For the moment, we just want to call attention to the positive side of this time of change. The examples we have given above show that the development of a second archetype can bring with it an important "broadening" or "balancing" effect. Midlife is often the time when this development begins to take place, and the result can be a richer and fuller life.

Look once more at the diagrams. The second or auxiliary archetype always appears to the right or left of your dominant archetype. No one jumps to the archetype that is opposite from his or her dominant archetype. For example, a Father does not find his second story in Seeker, and a Mediatrix does not become an Amazon. The reason for this was given at the beginning of this chapter. Opposite archetypes represent opposite priorities, opposite values, and such a different way of being that it is impossible to enter suddenly into the life of our opposite story.

But our opposite archetype does call for *attention* from time to time, especially in the second half of life. We cannot go through life blindly unaware of the values and priorities that are opposite to our own. In fact, it is a liberating thing to realize that the Great Story opposite to our own is just as legitimate and real as our own. This realization is often the beginning of true maturity.

We will return to the question of opposites later on. The point we want to make here is that our second or auxiliary archetype is never the story that is *opposite* to our dominant story. I can become more attentive to my opposite, I can come to appreciate it more, and I can gradually participate in portions of it. But I will never find my own identity and fulfillment *in* it. Life isn't long enough, and there just isn't time enough to do a total about-face regarding my basic way of seeing and going about things.

How many of the Great Stories can a person authentically live? Our answer is: one or two. No one ever lives three stories *fully* at the same time, much less four.

This answer does not come out of an abstract theory, but from our personal contact with hundreds of people who have shared their stories with us. Some writers suggest that we develop one archetype after another, gradually working our way around the whole circle.[1] This might sound possible and perhaps attractive. But even from the theoretical viewpoint there is a problem to which we have already alluded. Opposite archetypes represent opposite priorities and values, and it is difficult to see, even theoretically, how one person can find identity and fulfillment in *all* of the Great Stories within the compass of one lifetime.

In any case, this does not square with people's actual experience. After reflecting on the archetypes, mature men and women—including senior citizens—agree that they have indeed found their source of energy in one or two archetypes, no more. Again, keep in mind what we have been saying throughout this chapter: Everyone can find something of themselves in all of the stories. But it doesn't seem that life is long enough for any of us to find *identity and fulfillment* in more than two of the stories.

Note

1. E.g. Mario Moreno, "Archetypal Foundations in the Analysis of Women," *Journal of Analytical Psychology*, 10 (1965) 173–185; and Castillejo, *Knowing Woman*, p 70.

5

QUIRKS AND QUALITIES

It is a good thing we don't remember much from the first few years of our lives.

When we first emerge from the womb, we take leave of an ideal condition. During the first nine months of our existence, all of mother's physiological systems are directed toward nurturing us, step by intricate step. Her systems are so totally geared to the life in her womb that the infant can be affected by any of the drugs she ingests during pregnancy, and by any psychological trauma she might suffer. If all goes reasonably well, our days in the womb are the one time in our lives when all of our needs are satisfied: All systems are go. All of our hungers are fulfilled in a total way that we will never again experience in our lives.

Then we are launched into the world. And at some moment, somewhere amid our baby cries, we let out a primal scream when we got our first inkling that all those people out there exist for other reasons than our personal satisfaction. The womb was my personal paradise, and now that paradise is gone. I began life thinking (if I could think) that I am God. I began life as the center of the universe, because that is how it was when I was in the womb, with all systems working for me and me alone. Now my needs and hungers are connected with that whole vast world outside the womb.

The first few years of life are distressing, no matter how loving our parents are. Our needs at this stage are mostly physical and biological, and few of them are fulfilled as efficiently as they were in the womb. We have to cry before we get fed. We have to make noises before we get comfort and attention. And so we begin the long journey out of the unconscious paradise of the womb into the world of consciousness and self-awareness.

The word *systems* describes the focus of life in mother's

womb. This is an equally good word for describing our tasks and preoccupations in the first years of life outside the womb. We are born with a whole set of bodily systems that have to be brought into line and coordinated, from our bowel movements to the movements of our limbs and fingers. We also begin life surrounded by the systems of society: parents, family, community, all the forces that exercise authority over us. Our early awareness of the world is dominated by these two great "systems"—our own bodies, and the social structures that impinge on our daily existence. There is no need to go into detail here about the struggle and conflict that unfolds as we grow up and deal with these realities. Suffice it to say that we all go through our own personal purgatories and hells as we come to terms with our bodies and our parents, not to mention the world at large.

But whatever it might cost, everyone needs to develop a reasonably stable relationship with these systems. If we don't connect well with our own bodies, or if we are always in conflict with the basic social structures around us, it is simply impossible to get on with the other tasks of life.

We don't experience any of these "systems" abstractly. The first experience we have is that there are two kinds of people in the world: little people and big people. Big people are mothers and fathers. Not that all mothers and fathers are Mothers and Fathers in the archetypal sense. But we *experience* our parents archetypally because they nurture and provide and care for us. Before we know the least thing about our personal call or destiny, we are affected by the Great Stories of Mother and Father, and by whatever qualities and characteristics of these archetypes are found in our actual parents. All of our lives we will associate authority, even an ultimate kind of authority, with Mother and Father. They introduce us to social structure, and so they are the first and most powerful symbols of outer authority.

QUIRKS AND QUALITIES • 63

MOTHER AND FATHER

The archetypes of Mother and Father retain their initial power long after our childhood. In fact, these archetypes tend to overpower the other six. All eight of the Great Stories are separate, distinct, different—but equal. No one story is more valid than another. But because of our early experience of Mother and Father, and because they are protectors and nurturers in positions of authority, too often they appear as paragons of virtue or as the ultimate of the masculine and feminine.

A girl who is Mother and a boy who is Father start living out of their archetypes unconsciously at a very early age. They have role models which they can quickly identify with, and the values embodied in these archetypes are compatible with their way of being. Their own parents may not necessarily be Mother and Father in the archetypal sense, but the qualities and values of these archetypes are present in any kind of parenting, in fairy tales and children's stories, in the school system and in religion. Everyone has had the experience of being around a girl who is a "little mother." This illustrates the point we made earlier, that one does not have to be of a certain age or have children in order to be Mother or Father. We also mentioned that another person can identify our story even before we are conscious of living it.

Elizabeth is an attractive 22-year-old teacher in a junior high school. She is unmarried and has no children. During her first year of teaching, on the Friday before Mother's Day, she walked into her homeroom class and found it decorated with streamers and Mother's Day greetings. The class as a whole sensed that she was a Mother. The children were right. Elizabeth said afterward that she has consciously found identity and fulfillment in the Mother archetype ever since she was a little girl.

The word *consciously* is important here. Because Elizabeth is aware of the Great Story she is living, she has the ability to perceive the dark side as well as the bright side of her story. In her classroom, she has stopped moralizing on group responsibility and community effort, and she avoids the pitfalls of seeing her class as one big happy family. She has learned to be attentive to the needs of individual children, especially those who don't "need" her. At the same time, she is careful not to be overly protective of the frail student. These are all traps that the unconscious Mother easily falls into.

Elizabeth is not only conscious of her own story. She is also aware that there are other stories as legitimate as her own. Therefore she does not expect others to adopt her teaching style, and she is not judgmental about colleagues who have an approach to the classroom which is entirely different from her own—but equally effective.

Just as there is the "little mother," so there is the 10-year-old boy who is seen as the "man of the house." He readily assumes responsibility for himself and for others. From an early age he values the need for order. He has a strong sense of his place in the family and how he fits into the "system." As he gets older his horizons broaden, and as a young adult he is well tuned to the workings of the social structure. Father is leader, and from an early age he sees himself as a responsible member of the community: in his family, his Cub pack, his baseball team, his school.

An interesting situation arises when the parent of this young Father is not himself an archetypal Father, but another archetype, for example a Sage. By the time this little Father becomes a teenager, he is sensitive to a certain lack of order in his household. He might not be able to name it exactly, but things aren't being done around the house in the way he thinks they should be done. (This can also be true of a daughter who is Mother, but whose own mother is not a "Mother." Even at an early age, she will try to compensate for what she considers to be the lacks in her own parent.)

Kevin is the third son in a family of five children. His father is a Seeker and his mother is a Companion. Though happily mar-

ried, his parents never entirely grew up; all their lives they exhib-
ited the more immature qualities of their archetypes. As the
children were growing up, the atmosphere of the home was casual
and flexible, but also disorganized and at times chaotic. The children were habitually late for school, bills were not paid on time,
and leaking faucets rarely got fixed. By the time he was in his
teens, Kevin was keeping up the house and looking after his brothers and sisters (none of whom are Fathers or Mothers). He even
used his earnings from part-time jobs after school to pay his parents' delinquent utility bills. As a youth, Kevin found *identity* as
the Father in his family, but he experienced more frustration than
fulfillment in living this story. Fortunately, he has found this fulfillment in his own marriage and in fathering his own three children.

But unfortunately, circumstances have not allowed Kevin to
let go of his role of Father toward his parents and siblings. Christmas dinner is always at his house. In their fifties, his parents in-
herited several hundred thousand dollars. The inheritance would
have given them a very comfortable retirement—but they spent
the entire amount within a few years. Since then, Kevin's parents
have turned to him for loans to "see them through." He gets the
same requests from his brothers, who are constantly changing
their jobs and needing money to "tide them over." Despite their
ages (Kevin is the youngest person in this whole scenario), the entire family keeps turning to him as Father and provider.

Throughout history Father and Mother have been *favored*
stories. They are the most readily identifiable archetypes, and the
most strongly supported by society. As we suggested earlier, Mothers and Fathers have the advantage of being able to identify their
story at an early age. Because society supports these stories so
strongly, Fathers and Mothers can find *identity and fulfillment* in
their particular stories without much turmoil or tension. But at
the same time, because of the powerful support systems that surround these archetypes, Mothers and Fathers are often blind to

other ways of being and doing things—in fact, six other ways that are as valid and valuable as their way.

More than any other archetype, Mothers and Fathers run the risk of not being able to admit to their own deficiencies and weaknesses. Ironically enough, even when they want to become conscious of their limitations, people of other archetypes tend to protect them from unpleasant truths about themselves. Mother and Father enjoy a special immunity. No one wants to hurt Mother's feelings or incur Father's wrath. Everyone needs a Father and Mother, and many people spend years of their lives in search of the ideal parent. As a result, society generally idealizes these archetypes more than any of the others. We are all familiar with the saying "Father knows best." The same cultural attitude pertains to Mother as well. Men who are Father and women who are Mother have to be very careful not to become inflated with the myths and idealized projections which are laid onto these archetypes. On the other hand, many Fathers and Mothers are only too well aware of their shortcomings, and are burdened by the idealization of society and of their own children.

Fathers, and Mothers even more so, are drawn to be the spokesperson for the young, the weak, and the underprivileged. They become the buffer between the world of "they" out there and the warmth of the hearth. Often this is necessary and helpful. However, because Mothers and Fathers find identity and fulfillment in this consoling and supportive role, they sometimes take charge when help is not needed or required. Too often a passing comment from the distressed can lead them into battle unnecessarily. Mother and Father must be careful to acquaint themselves with both sides of the story. They should encourage tattling children to deal with their own problems responsibly. When they are among adults, Mother and Father are the most likely to fall prey to whiners who are unwilling to take charge of their own lives.

Mothers and Fathers tend to take themselves and their tasks quite seriously. This is true whether they are five or fifty years of age. Their sense of responsibility is a great gift to any family or community—but they also need a sense of humor to put life into perspective. In social settings, some Mothers and Fathers find it difficult to carry on a casual conversation which is unrelated to their roles of nurturing, caring, and providing for their brood. If they cannot facilitate things in an official way, they don't know what to do with themselves. If they cannot preside over the gathering or be of service to others, they often sit silently on the sidelines, feeling helpless or looking uncomfortably idle.

Novelist Dick Francis gives a good portrait of the Father who seems unable to have genuine peer relationships.

> In some ways I knew Trevor no better than on that first day. Our real relationship began and ended at the office door, social contact outside being confined to one formal dinner party each year, to which I was invited by letter by his wife. . . . Friends tended to be top management types or county councilors, worthy substantial citizens like Trevor himself. On the professional level, I knew him well. Orthodox establishment outlook, somber and traditional. Patriarchal, but not pompous. Giving the sort of gilt-edged advice that still appears sound even if in hindsight it turned out not to be. Something punitive about him, perhaps. He seemed to me sometimes to get a positive pleasure from detailing the extent of a client's tax liabilities, and watching the client droop. Precise in mind and method, discreetly ambitious, pleased to be a noted local personage, and at his charming best with rich old ladies.[1]

It does not seem possible that the power of Father or Mother could be dislodged by any cultural changes. Their roles are simply so basic to the structure of society. Though there has been a shift of attention to Amazon, Mother still retains her original power. However, the cultural developments of modern society have profoundly affected the Father archetype. Father is King. That is how he is depicted in the ancient myths, where he is the ruler and leader who holds authority over all. But in our day, Father has been dethroned from his kingly state.

Father used to be the only breadwinner, the only provider in the family. He had the final word on the education of the children and their choice of a profession. Now his wife is his equal, both legally and economically. Father used to see it as a matter of pride to be able to provide a dowry for his daughters, a place in his business for his sons, and an inheritance for all of his children. Now the children are less interested in what Father can provide, especially if it might stifle their own independence. The children have good reason to feel independent when they leave home and take a job. Many of the securities that Father alone once supplied, such as care in times of illness or unemployment, are now provided by the state.

Father has thus been dethroned from his position of kingship in the family, both by his wife and by the state. The church has also eroded Father's position as king of the family. The Christian churches used to preach that the father's authority over his family is a reflection of the ultimate authority of God the heavenly Father. Today, theology is not inclined to project the makings of the patriarchal system onto God, take the image of God as Father literally or anthropomorphically, and then justify the patriarchy by saying that God made it. Except for fundamentalists, most Christian churches are alive to the dangers of identifying the human Father with the image of God the Father. So Father has also been dethroned by religion.

These cultural changes have made Father insecure and unsure of his role. In the past, he did not have to listen to his children's points of view, or even those of his wife. Now his wife and children may accuse him of being aloof or rigid or close-minded. Often his children aren't even interested in the truths and values that he learned from his own father. They have no sense of tradition, no respect for social convention, and they are unwilling to meet any of the expectations that he thinks are reasonable.

What is worse, he knows that his children's attitudes are supported by the spirit of the times, and this makes him feel all the more helpless and impotent. Father's frustration finds two different outlets. It may turn into violence, so that he batters his family, physically or emotionally. Or he may withdraw entirely and become a non-entity, too weak to be respected. [2]

AMAZON AND WARRIOR

After Father and Mother, the stories that are most likely to catch a child's attention are Warrior and Amazon. The reason for this is that the qualities and values embodied in these Great Stories are highly respected by the "systems" we have to deal with from our earliest years. Mother and Father themselves tend to respect and support the Warrior and Amazon more strongly than they do the other archetypes.

By the time they reach school age, both girls and boys are caught up in the Warrior-Amazon world of achievement, competition, and the drive for independence. This is true both in the classroom and on the playground. At an early age, some children are invigorated by this atmosphere while others become discouraged. Or resistant. One mother recounted her experience of jogging with her two small sons. They go out to a park several times a week. One of the two boys is determined to beat her in the race around the park track. Her other son is not interested in the competition: he runs in the other direction.

Amazons and Warriors need recognition for themselves and their activities in a way that the Sage and Mediatrix do not. From the time they are very young, they collect and display badges and emblems of their achievements (Mother and Father take pride in these awards). This practice continues into adulthood. If honored or degreed, Amazons and Warriors are the most likely to use titles before their names and initials after. When you enter their home or office, it is obvious that their certificates and trophies are cherished. A Sage or a Mediatrix could possess similar emblems of achievement, but they are usually stored in a box in the basement, or if they are on display they need dusting.

There has always been an arena for the Warrior. We only need to look at myths, folklore, and contemporary children's literature, including comic books, to realize that men who live the Warrior archetype have always had an opportunity to find identity and fulfillment in it. On the other hand, while the *qualities* of the Amazon have always been valued, *woman* as Amazon has not always been appreciated. She figures prominently enough in the ancient myths, but until quite recently she has not been a key figure in modern children's literature. Comic books gave us Sheena of the Jungle and Wonder Woman, but unless you had the right bust measurement it was difficult to identify with such women. Aside from someone like Nancy Drew, or Astrid Lindgren's Pippi Longstocking, most portrayals of Amazons stressed the negative side of this archetype.

There has been a dramatic change in the last decade. Women's magazines have shifted their focus from Mother in the home to Amazon in the marketplace, including the stock-marketplace. This has given freedom to Amazon women who have felt trapped by home and family. These are the women who need a larger arena than the home if they are to find happiness. Many have been Supermoms who have meticulously managed their household, but are more frustrated than fulfilled. Their management of the home tends to concentrate on the physical needs rather than the emotional needs of the members of the family. In their frustration they can become demanding and bitter. By midlife, they need space from the home—and their family needs space from them. They need to put their energies to the service of larger causes than the household. Many Amazons enter the business world or public life and are energized by the broader challenge.

Lois is an Amazon who once claimed the title Supermom.

She was a gourmet cook who did her own canning, and a seamstress who made all her children's clothes. She refinished the furniture, she did all the painting and wallpapering, and she drove her children back and forth from dancing lessons and hockey games. She convened her church bazaar, and in general prided herself on the way she organized everyone's time. Her three children, who are now adults, remember how she would wake them in the middle of the night to tidy their closets and toy boxes. Her husband earned a steady income and was happy in his job, but Lois saw him as lacking ambition, and she considered it her duty to push him ahead. No matter how much her husband tried to understand her and help around the house, his efforts were always criticized. (Most mother-in-law jokes and barbs are aimed at the dark side of Amazon-Mother, and for good reason.)

Lois' children left home immediately after high school because the tension in the home and the pressure to achieve was simply too much. Lois gradually realized that all of the things she did "for others" were primarily done to keep herself occupied or to gain recognition. She came to the conclusion that for everyone's sake, including her own, she had to set goals for herself outside the home. Things have in fact turned out well for her. Lois was elected to the city council, where she has served several terms. Her keen mind and her leadership abilities are respected in the community. Relationships with her husband and her children have improved as she has withdrawn her ambitious projections from them and achieved in her own right. Her house, which was once the focal point of her existence, is not as tidy as it used to be, but this doesn't bother Lois anymore.

Lois gives us an example of a purposeful woman who felt frustrated until she got outside the home. She lacked a sufficient cause or mission on which to focus her energies, and she had to suppress a whole portion of her being that needed an outlet.

The feminist movement is a plea for recognition and support of the Amazon story. It is certainly time that women be treated justly, and their contributions to society should be recognized. But because recognition of the Amazon story is so long overdue, many women of this archetype over-react.

Ellen, armed with her latest degree in social work, is exasperated with her younger sister who has given up a promising career to be at home with her two young children. Ellen is not very calm or self-contained; she is aggressive and openly competitive in her relationships with others. Unconsciously she has adopted traits which she criticizes in men. At social gatherings, when she is introduced to other women, her first question is usually "And what do *you* do?" She defines "accomplishment" almost exclusively in terms of her own Amazon story, and one gets the impression that in Ellen's eyes other women are only as good as their latest accomplishment. Ellen is not unlike many militant women, active in the feminist movement, who place so much emphasis on woman as Amazon that they overlook the equal rights of the other three feminine stories, and thus treat other women unjustly.

Cliff is the founder and president of a company that manufactures equipment for the oil industry. He is a Warrior and a classic example of the self-made man. His success in business has brought him prominence in public life. Now in his fifties, Cliff enjoys giving time to his various positions on civic committees and the boards of charitable organizations. He is generous with his own wealth. He contributes quietly and without notoriety to many causes.

Among his activities, Cliff is a member of the Board of Governors of the state university in his area. A few years ago, the professors at the university were negotiating for a raise in pay that would make their salaries more commensurate with the earnings of professional people in the private sector. In a television interview on the evening news, Cliff explained why he was opposed to any significant jump in pay for the professors. "If they were worth that kind of money," he said, "they would be out here in the real world where the action is." Despite his generosity, when it comes to *earning* money, Cliff defines achievement strictly in terms of his own archetype, and he is not prepared to give awards for accomplishments that differ from his own. Happily, there were other people than Cliff on the Board of Governors, and the professors got a small raise.

There is a new breed of Amazons and Warriors who have learned from their bitter older brothers and sisters. They strive to have a balanced lifestyle. They are attentive to their health, to quality time with their spouses and children, and to the values inherent in the other Great Stories. Attempting to achieve the ideal balance energizes them—thus creating another goal for them.

All four of the archetypes that we have been looking at in this chapter have an important characteristic in common. Father and Mother, Warrior and Amazon all have an inborn appreciation for social order and hierarchical structure. To use a spatial image, they experience life *vertically*. They need order and structure, a sense of top and bottom, in order to know where they fit in the scheme of things and thus function effectively.

The saying "It's not what you know but whom you know" expresses a philosophy that is common to these four archetypes. These are the people who are best at *networking*. They know how the world is run and who runs it. They are sensitive to social conventions and skilled in using roles to their best advantage. They admire others who are equally skilled. They promote the idea of having good connections, and if they are parents they encourage their children to have the right friends. What the "right" connections are will be defined on the basis of achievement, or character, or religion, etc.

The remaining four archetypes—Sage and Mediatrix, Seeker and Companion—experience life *horizontally*. They are more interested in knowledge and one-to-one relationships than in competition and achievement. They are well enough aware of roles and social structures, but they are rarely preoccupied with these "vertical" dimensions of life. Amazon-Warrior and Mother-Father often see this lack of interest as a lack of purpose or a waste of talent. In their eyes, Sage and Mediatrix, Seeker and Companion may appear to be unrealistic, impractical, and naive about how the world works.

These are indeed the quirks of many a Seeker and Companion, Sage and Mediatrix. But these archetypes also have their positive qualities.

Notes

1. Dick Francis, *Risk* (Pocket Books, 1977), p 6.
2. Vera von der Heydt, "The Personal Father" (London: Guild Spring Conference, 1978), pp 7–8. Same author, "On the Father in Psychotherapy," in *Fathers and Mothers* (Spring Publications, 1973), pp 128–142.

6

MORE QUIRKS AND QUALITIES

"Wisdom begins when acquaintance with your own odd quirks equals your estimate of the over-all queerness of everyone else."[1] Good words, worth pondering. This chapter will talk about the quirks and qualities of the remaining four archetypes.

Mother and Father, Amazon and Warrior tend to be *least aware* of other stories than their own. Sometimes they are reluctant to recognize that any other stories can be "Great" Stories. Sage and Mediatrix, Seeker and Companion are only *too well aware* that there are many legitimate ways of being. This awareness is at once a blessing and a curse.

SEEKER AND COMPANION

In her song "The Altruist and the Needy Case," Dory Previn draws a wonderful sketch of the Seeker, his blessing and his curse, his bright and dark sides.

he has passion
for ecology
compassion
for minorities
he carries printed placards
to put an end to war
he's a hero
he's a rebel
with a half a hundred causes
he peddles his petitions
door to door . . .

he writes letters

to his congressman
on indian indignities
black men
are his brothers
he bears collective guilt
he's a prophet
he's a pacifist . . .

his roots are with the rootless
that's where he needs to be
he will die
with total strangers
but he will not live
with me . . .

he's a seeker
he's a saviour
who strives to
save the children
but he's never had
a child of his own

he's united
with the universe
he's at one
with stars and sea
he can love
the whole damned human race
oh
then why is he
so afraid to be
in love with me?[2]

Seekers often lead a stormy life in their search for identity and
peace of mind. As the song so eloquently says, their ideals and
good intentions can get in the way of close relationships, not to

mention stable or long-term commitments. The Eternal Boy who has never grown up is easily caricatured.

But there is also the mature Seeker who is not a Peter Pan and who is not ruled by his wanderlust.

Like many Seekers, Greg took his time finding his place in life. He quit college several times, once in order to travel around Europe, and another time in order to take a job and get some experience of life. He had begun university with the intention of becoming a doctor. When he finally graduated, he had a bachelor's degree in history and no intention of doing anything further with it. He took a job selling insurance and did well with the company, advancing within a few years to a position in management. When he was thirty, Greg quit the insurance company and opened a shop that sells second-hand books. Greg has had his bookstore for ten years now, and he is content in what he is doing. As it turns out, his business even pulls together some apparently unconnected threads from his earlier life, such as his travels and his degree in history.

Greg's parents had never put any pressure on him, but they admit that they kept their fingers crossed while he was wandering about during his twenties. Seekers often do not end up doing what they set out to do in the beginning. What may appear to others as detours and blind alleys are usually a necessary part of the Seeker's journey. The Seeker who is also a Sage tends to be a perennial pupil, the career student. This was tempting for Greg, but he decided to test his knowledge in the wider world.

Greg did not marry until he was almost thirty. He had his own experience of the Eternal Boy's tendency to "love 'em and leave 'em," and he was determined not to marry until he was sure that he could live with the commitment. He and his wife have one child. Greg's archetype is opposite to that of Father, and he had never felt in himself the "need" to have children that Fathers and Mothers experience. The first years of his son David's life were a difficult time for Greg. He and his wife liked to take off and do interesting things, and Greg felt tied down by the daily schedule that surrounds the care of an infant. He did not experience instant paternal feelings toward his newborn son.

David is now ten years old, and Greg has related to him more and more as each year has passed. He is excited by any of David's blossoming interests, and he likes to share his hobbies with his son. The toys he buys for David tend to tie in with his own current hobbies. Greg likes to make things out of wood, and he has been disappointed a few times when David has not shown much enthusiasm for the tools his dad bought for him. But Greg is aware that his son should be exposed to interests other than his own. Last summer he made arrangements for David to spend a few weeks with his uncle—who happens to be a Father, and who is paternal toward David in a way that Greg knows he cannot be.

The Seeker archetype describes an authentic way of being, just as legitimate as Father or Warrior. This archetype is not a stage *toward* something else. It is one of the Great Stories in its own right. As we indicated in Chapter 3, and as Greg's story illustrates, the Eternal Boy who does grow up into a mature Seeker has powerful positive qualities about him. But it seems to take him more time to bring his positive qualities to maturity. This is probably the reason why society doesn't grant this archetype the same status it gives to Father or Warrior.

We are all familiar with the feminine form of Dory Previn's altruist. This free woman appears to be self-contained and purposeful. She wants to be, indeed needs to be, where the action is. On the surface, the altruistic Companion resembles the Amazon. But a closer look reveals that she lacks the Amazon woman's focus and single-mindedness.

This Companion lives in a world of possibilities, and each new relationship presents more possibilities. Often she squanders her energies by getting involved too quickly. Her discernment process seems to take place *in* the involvement and *within* the relating. Her current causes and activities are usually inspired by a new relationship, or else they are an escape from the last one. This woman is willing to take part in almost anything that comes her way. She might not experience any limitations until midlife. If she does not bring her Companion nature to consciousness and acknowledge realistic limitations, she will never be capable of commitment. She will bring harm to those whom she sets out to help.

In F. Scott Fitzgerald's story "The Last of the Southern Belles," we meet another kind of Companion. This one is the feminine version of the Eternal Boy, namely the Eternal Girl. She is the sweet young thing who gets her identity from the admiration and projections of others. She luxuriates in an exciting lifestyle where she is all-powerful without any effort on her own part, and where all of her whims are satisfied. This artificial environment provides her with such instant identity that she is never prompted to wonder who she is. She is whatever her latest beau wants her to be. Fulfillment for her is simply having her identity as a Southern belle. In another culture she might find her identity in being Doctor's wife or the woman beside the Famous Man.

Blissfully passive, the belle-Companion gradually exchanges her independence for a comfortable life where she is dependent on others for constant affirmation. Being a young "thing" she has no personal identity of her own. She doesn't grow up; she simply grows older. The aging sweet young thing is a pitiful person. The once charming woman whose potential is wasted not by anyone else, but by her own weakness, is truly a tragic heroine. This is the story of many women who find themselves alone through divorce or the death of their husband. They never realized to what extent they identified themselves with their husband's personality or profession. Paradoxically, it may be only through their being *alone* that they finally become aware of their Companion nature.

Companions who are altruists and those who are Eternal Girls have a common characteristic: Their activities and relationships have more intensity to them than depth or permanence.

Some Companions consciously choose not to have any identity separate from their relationship to the man they love. Cynthia Koestler is an extreme example of this kind of Companion. In 1949 she became the secretary of Hungarian-born writer Arthur Koestler, author of *Darkness at Noon* and other bestsellers. She was his devoted companion and lover for many years before he finally consented to marry her in 1965. Her adoration of Arthur prevented her from seeing the relationship objectively. He was a womanizer, a heavy drinker, and an intellectual bully. Despite his faults, her devotion was so strong that she could not bear the thought of a day passing without knowing what his opinions were.

Arthur was over 75, suffering from Parkinson's disease and leukemia, when he committed suicide in March of 1983. Cynthia, 55 years old and in good health, joined her husband in his death by taking her own life. She had never really lived her own story. When Arthur chose to end his life, Cynthia's life was over as well.

The immature Companion has difficulty with boundaries and limitations. The idealistic Companion refuses to acknowledge any realistic boundaries, for fear they might cramp her style. The clinging Companion on the other hand creates limits that don't really exist in order to protect herself from the real world and from the discomfort of coming to terms with who she really is.[3]

MEDIATRIX AND SAGE

Contemporary western culture provides few role models for the Mediatrix. When people read the description of the mediumistic woman, they are inclined to think of Greek goddesses, witches, or psychics. But there are many women who identify with this story, and they are relieved to learn that they are not alone.

Lynne is one such woman. From the time she was a child,

she felt caught between the tangible present and something that was much more enveloping. Her access to the collective unconscious both enriched her and confused her. She was fascinated by a certain cosmic relatedness, but at the same time she was overwhelmed by its implications and by her place in the scheme of things. Lynne was filled with a sense of purpose on one day and a feeling of worthlessness on the next.

One of the things that often bewildered her was her uncanny knowledge of other people. She found herself trusting women whom others scorned, and having doubts about men whom others admired. Lynne assumed that everyone had similar insights, and she wondered why they didn't act on them. Indifferent as she was to status and social convention, she often voiced her impressions publicly without fully realizing the consequences of her action. In fact, she often found herself surprised by what she was saying out loud, and wondered where it came from.

In school, Lynne got above-average grades. She was intelligent and artistic, but not at all motivated by competition or recognition. She would put hours into her projects, and walk away from them as soon as someone else recognized her ability. When she won an art award she wasn't in attendance. Others were surprised or annoyed by her lack of ambition. Lynne herself was baffled by her own behavior.

Unable to set goals for herself, Lynne was vague about her future upon graduation from high school. After a series of short-term jobs, she entered college and took a variety of art and English courses. She left college without a degree and accepted the first "people" job she could find, working as a medical receptionist. She spent her free time reading, sculpting, and painting. For Lynne, art was a way of expressing in the outer world what she was receiving within. It was only when things could be transferred to some tangible medium that she felt she had some control over them and could give them form. Contact with the unconscious evoked from her a different way of seeing. One would not describe her work as abstract, but it is symbolic. There is an un-self-conscious flow to her art; nothing is contrived or gimmicky.

As a young woman, when meeting someone for the first time, Lynne often experienced positive impulses, or on the other hand a sense of disruption. She learned not to voice all of her impressions immediately, and if her thoughts were negative she felt guilty about them. She was not a superstitious person, but could not help wondering where her thoughts were coming from. She felt exonerated when time and circumstances revealed that her initial impressions were correct. But this didn't stop her from questioning her motives—or her sanity—whenever these incidents occurred.

Lynne had realized in grade school that certain friendships helped her to focus and motivated her to set goals for herself. In her late twenties, she was still trying to find identity and stability through one-on-one relationships that would stimulate her to develop her gifts in a disciplined way. She had good friendships with a variety of men and women. Lynne married in her early thirties and had three children. She thought that being a mother would give her an identity and bring her some kind of fulfillment. She remembers the first nine years of child-rearing as a time when she lived in "a foggy vacuum filled with noise and confusion." Still, her children did not distract her from experimenting with different art forms and from spending time alone with her husband.

Through community activities Lynne made the acquaintance of men who, from time to time, would come to talk to her. She was friendly and extraverted but didn't consider herself a flirt. Nor was she a psychologist. Some of these conversations made her wonder why the man was talking to her instead of to a counselor or a close friend. Over a period of years a curious pattern emerged. Either in person or by letter, she was the last one to have contact with a number of men before they died. A few times she was aware of her role, but usually she was not. In one instance a young priest asked her to "accompany him into death." He died within the year. Throughout all of this, the love of her sensible husband was an anchor for her, and Lynne counted on him for direction and support.

Uncontrolled and undirected thoughts and impressions, images and notions governed her days, and often her nights. Lynne's children were getting older, and her husband was becoming weary of her unfocused lifestyle. She had difficulty recognizing the fruits of her endeavors. She thought she had wasted her time and talent, and had neglected the needs of her children by not being a nurturing mother.

In midlife Lynne struggled to name things for herself and to give some shape to her life. She came to appreciate that her "sixth sense" is as natural to her as an ear for music or an eye for color is to someone else. With this realization her particular way of "knowing" things, which had been a distraction and a burden all her life, now became a gift to be developed and no longer denied. She decided, while keeping up with her art work, to set some boundaries for herself and to resist wasting her energies on every intriguing insight. A combination of circumstances and a conscious decision on her part led her to become interested in graphoanalysis. After years of research and study in the field of handwriting analysis, Lynne has become a resource person for a number of corporations, and she is often consulted by the police. At the age of fifty, she has finally found identity and fulfillment in her Mediatrix archetype by discovering an outlet for her mediumistic ways.

Both Mediatrix and Amazon are less motivated by a need to please others than are Mother and Companion. This gives them an independence not enjoyed by Mother and Companion. But as Lynne's story illustrates, mediumistic women need help from the Mother or Companion story to maintain stability in their lives while they go about the task of developing the strong ego that is necessary to become a positive Mediatrix. The nurturing activities of Mother, or the Companion's experiences of accompanying and being accompanied, provide the Mediatrix with some identity and

fulfillment while she goes about this task. The Mediatrix archetype is related to the impersonal world of the unconscious, while
Mother and Companion are ways of relating personally to others.
These archetypes help to "ground" the Mediatrix and enable her
to sort out what belongs to the world of symbol and images, and
what belongs to the reality of here and now.

If she protects and cares for others as Mother, the Mediatrix
must be careful not to pass confusion and turmoil onto those in
her care. She has to remain attentive to her Mediatrix story and
not use Mother's activities as a permanent refuge. Similarly, if she
finds some identity and support in the Companion's way of being,
she must be on guard that she doesn't lose her ego in the personality of the one she loves. These are strong temptations for the
mediumistic woman. Once she gets involved in activities that offer some temporary fulfillment, she can too easily set aside the task
that is difficult but necessary for her, namely, developing a strong
ego and discovering her own identity as Mediatrix.

Leonard Cohen gives us an example of the unfocused Mediatrix-Companion in his portrait of Suzanne who "takes you
down to her place by the river."

> You can hear the boats go by,
> You can stay the night beside her.
> And you know that she's half crazy
> But that's why you want to be there,
> And she feeds you tea and oranges
> That come all the way from China
> And just when you want to tell her
> That you have no love to give her,
> Then she gets you on her wave length
> And she lets the river answer
> That you've always been her lover
>
> And you want to travel with her,
> And you want to travel blind

And you think you maybe trust her
'Cause she's touched your perfect body
With her mind.[4]

If people are happy in their jobs, they have undoubtedly found one which harmonizes with their Great Story, a job in which they can live out significant aspects of their story.

This is also true for the Sage. He is not found only in institutions of higher learning or scientific laboratories where he is pushing back the boundaries of knowledge. The Sage is also the handyman who, after he has finished working on your kitchen cabinets, talks to you about the latest books he has read.

The Sage is the missionary who went abroad to help people in a third world country, and made his biggest contribution by helping them to gather and write down the herbal remedies and folk medicines of their people.

The Sage is the executive of a construction company who sponsors educational programs for his employees—not courses in construction or engineering, but programs dealing with personal growth and self-understanding.

The Sage is the high-school science teacher who has been offered more lucrative jobs in industry, but knows he would be lost if he could not teach young people how the cosmos is put together.

The Sage is the old British gentleman who, when asked if he had change for a pound, gave a history of the British monetary system along with his coins of shillings and pence.

Sages love to explain things. The Sage who is a piano-tuner is not likely to let you go after he has finished his tuning job. He will want you to *understand* the adjustments he made on the hammers, how the action of the keys works, and why humidity affects the felts. When Sages are explaining things, their listeners are often tapping their toes or looking at their watches, at least mentally. (Many people wish they could get a few good Sage-style explanations from their doctor, their dentist, and their auto mechanic.)

Many Sages are good with words, and they know how to put complex ideas together. But sometimes the Sage can get so caught up in the intriguing connections he finds between one idea and another, one theory and another, that he forgets what he set out to explain. The dark side of this archetype emerges even more when the Sage does not really possess the knowledge or wisdom to which he lays claim. Then he is likely to conceal his ignorance in a web of rhetoric that sounds learned but says nothing.

Gerald is a former university professor who is now a consultant for a research foundation. He wrote several books which criticized the practices and operating principles of the educational system and of the health professions. The books received wide acclaim. On the whole, Gerald told his readers what they already knew: many things are far from perfect in schools and hospitals. But his books were very readable, they contained interesting information, and they went right for the Achilles' heel of institutions with which everyone has to cope.

Like every author who has published best-sellers, Gerald gets invitations to give talks. Recently a large university invited him to give a lecture as part of its Distinguished Lectures series. Gerald's field of interest had shifted to ecology, and so he decided to lecture on the ways that Western nations have exploited nature and endangered the globe. Gerald was again taking on large institutions—nations this time—which are highly vulnerable and open to attack. His topic was a safe one for a university-sponsored lecture, and it was sure to generate interest in the wider community. People who had reservations about the scholarly soundness of Gerald's books wondered about his new expertise in ecology. But the topic was current and interesting, the speaker had a big name, and tickets for the lecture were quickly sold out.

Some five hundred people assembled for the event. Gerald, always a clever speaker, began by explaining the amount of energy generated by a lioness in heat and how much lion-energy it took to fly him to the lecture. He then talked about the etymology of the word "ecology," which is rooted in the Greek word for "house." This took him into "economics," which has the same root, and he went on to discourse about the history of economic development and the use of money for trade. Apparently returning to ecology, he described how waste was disposed of during the Middle Ages in northern Europe. And so the lecture went on, and on, and on.

Halfway into the lecture, it was obvious that Gerald had interesting information and a way with words, but nothing to say. One man in the audience whispered to his wife, "If he finishes by ten o'clock I can go home and watch Barney Miller." But many people leaving the lecture were heard to say, "Wasn't that exciting? Gerald just knows so *much!*"

It was clearly a case of the emperor's clothes. That is the way it often is with Sages who are more clever than wise.

Notes

1. Maria Mahoney, *The Meaning in Dreams and Dreaming* (Citadel Press, 1966), p 79.
2. Copyright 1971, Mediarts Music Inc./Bouquet Music.
3. Linda Leonard, "Puella Patterns," *Psychological Perspectives* (Fall 1978), pp 127–143.
4. R. Goldstein (ed.), *The Poetry of Rock* (Bantam, 1968), p 82.

7

OPPOSITES

Clare's invitation reads December 27, from 2 to 6 P.M. So you decide to drop in at her Christmas party around four. You wonder if it will be the usual circus. Clare, 32, is a vibrant Companion whose annual open house is always a collection of people from the past year's adventures. You never know what to expect at one of her gatherings.

Always the charming hostess, Clare greets you with enthusiasm and leads you into a room filled with animated voices and festive music. Faces turn your way, and you try not to appear too aloof or too eager as you are introduced to the assembly. The faces register reactions before you have opened your mouth and said a word.

Suddenly Clare whisks you away to meet the new man in her life. Fred is fatherly, a silver-haired 55. Quiet yet warm, he impresses you immediately as being stable and sensible. You are happily surprised by her choice this time.

After a minute or so Clare leaves you in mid-sentence as she dashes to the door to welcome Randy, who has just flown in from El Salvador. You and the entire staff at the office have heard all about Randy. Clare met him while vacationing in Greece last summer. He was that "marvelous man" who talked about "spatial freedom" and who was concerned about the invasion of other people's territory. Fred sarcastically muses that he is probably a part-time vegetarian. In his forties, Randy is showing signs of wear. His faded jeans and Kennedy button seem a little out of place, and you wonder if he changes his shorts once a week.

Clare introduces Randy—and Randy turns to introduce everyone to the wonderful woman he met on the plane. Your hostess is surprised and a little miffed, and it shows. Amy is a waif in cotton, and she is all too familiar. You've met women like her before: no matter what their age, they always seem a little vague and innocently eccentric. Randy and Amy complement each other. Both are indifferent to the practical and the utilitarian, and they seem to have some far-reaching mission. You muse that they will probably prop up each other's vision for a few months.

The decorated buffet is spread with every holiday goodie imaginable. Clare is off in a corner, "sharing" an intense conversation with Warren. Every so often she looks up and reminds all the guests to help themselves. Clare had made a resolution to herself to be more present to her guests this year. But Warren is new in town and doesn't know anyone else at the party. He recently opened a car dealership, and Clare met him when she was thinking about a new car. One thing led to another, and so Warren found himself at Clare's annual party. Warren is a 35-year-old entrepreneur from Illinois who has established himself locally, in his words, by "conquering the territory" and by being "on the offensive in these tough economic times."

Randy bristles as he overhears snatches of Warren's conversation. Tired from traveling, he decides not to get into an argument with Warren over oppression and ethics. He wanders across the room and sits next to Sloane, who has just flunked out of law school and is now working for the post office. Amy follows Randy and sits on the floor. Sloane is explaining how the complex economic problems of the third world countries directly affect the monetary affairs of Europe and North America and the price of panty-hose. People drift in and out of this circle of conversation. Most people can only take ten minutes of Sloane in one sitting.

Randy is very interested in Sloane's ideas. He contributes first-hand information of his own as he relates some of his personal experiences. One idea generates another, and soon the two men are oblivious to everyone else. Amy pretends to understand the conversation, which has now lost everyone else.

Fred interrupts Warren and Clare to find out where she keeps the large coffee pot. You take advantage of the break in their conversation to compliment Clare on the delicious antipasto. Clare calls to her friend Meg and passes the compliment on. As usual, Meg has done most of the baking and much of the preparation for Clare's party. Meg is an old classmate of hers, and one of the few faces that is familiar to you. It seems Meg has always been there for Clare. She has picked up after many of her parties, and after a few of her broken engagements.

Meg takes a drink over to Amy, who hasn't stirred from her place at Randy's feet. She picks up the empty glasses and asks Clare if there are any clean dishtowels. Clare is now wrapped up in a conversation with a couple who recently moved into the apartment across the hall. Clare leaves Fred and Meg to introduce the few late arrivals, and she trusts that all the guests will look after themselves. Warren decides that Amy needs some looking after, and he goes over to talk to her. He wouldn't want her working in his office, but something about her intrigues him.

Meg and Fred go out to the kitchen to put some order into the chaos there. They both marvel at the way Clare functions in the midst of such confusion. As they talk about Clare, they find themselves speaking of her as though she were their child. Fred has to remind himself that Clare is Meg's age. She is an adult. Fred is a widower, and his relationship with Clare has given him a new lease on life, but Clare's unpredictable ways and flexible lifestyle are unsettling to him. Meg is not the exciting woman that Clare is, but he feels comfortable working alongside her as they prepare coffee and tea for the guests.

Alex (short for Alexandra) bursts into the living room. She has just closed the biggest real-estate deal of her young career and she is flying high. Everyone notices Alex. Amy was overwhelmed by her presence the minute she walked through the door. Alex introduces herself to the group, and she quickly senses a few potential clients in the room. Sloane is a little unnerved by her forthrightness, but admires her sense of purpose and self-confidence. Warren feels challenged by this independent woman. The women in the room at once love her or hate her. No one reacts neutrally to Alex. Meg invites everyone to have tea or coffee before driving home.

On her way over to the buffet Alex takes you aside and asks about "aimless Amy." Women like Amy infuriate her. Alex was born with a purpose and a goal, she explains, and she will never get the respect she has earned for herself so long as "spacy ladies like that are simply content with existing."

It is late. With all the performances that have gone on, including your own, you are tired. Most of the people in the room have met you for the first time. There has been no chance for you to get to know anyone. You have responded positively to some people, you have reacted negatively to others. As you get your coat, you wonder why. Fred helps you on with your coat, and you wonder how other people have experienced *you*.

No chance to catch Clare alone to say goodbye. Not to worry. Fred will convey the message. You know you will hear from her soon. So will everyone else. A personable phone call, or a few lines on unique stationery, will explain and apologize for her lack of attentiveness today. You get the same message from Clare every January.

You walk to your car and vow not to accept next year's invitation. But you know you will.

Why is it that we can walk into a roomful of people and experience an instant dislike for someone we haven't even met or talked to? And why is it that, in the same room, there is another person who intrigues us even before we have heard the sound of his or her voice?

What is at work here is the psychological mechanism called *projection*. People usually use this word in its pejorative or negative sense. "Don't project your problems onto other people," we say. Or "I think you're projecting your own insecurity onto Jack." This negative aspect is real enough, but projection is also one of the most important ways in which we *find out about ourselves.* Projection has to do with the fact that we do not first experience our own inner qualities within ourselves. We first see them in other people, who mirror back to us the qualities that lie within ourselves.

A four-year-old boy knows very little about the world and less about himself. But if he does not *know* his inner potential, he is already *experiencing* it through his projections onto his heroes: his father perhaps, or his older brother, or the boy next door who is tougher than the other kids on the block. The life of every child and adolescent is filled with heroes and heroines, people who represent to us the human qualities and achievements that are most attractive to us. We have to go through the process of identifying with heroes and the ideals they represent before we can decide which of these qualities to make our own. I have my own inner strengths and resources. But there is no way they can be tested by the fire of experience unless I have first recognized, through projection and hero-worship, *which* strengths and resources are worth the struggle.

This is the positive side of "projection" which is often overlooked. The reason it is overlooked is that by the time we enter adulthood, we have probably had too many discomfiting experiences of the negative side of this mechanism. We have learned that our heroes and heroines are not what our projections made them out to be. They turn out to be real rather than ideal people, and they have faults and shortcomings like our own.

It is eventually a relief to know this about the people whom we have idealized, but the discovery is devastating at first. This is true especially when we are young, but it remains true throughout our lives. It is always upsetting to discover that our idols have clay feet. Perhaps the most discomforting part of the discovery is that the problem lies in ourselves and not in the other person, who may never have wanted to bear our idealized projections in the first place. When others are aware that I am idealizing them, they might try to discourage me by pointing out their deficiencies. If I persist in my projection, I will think they are being humble or falsely modest.

By the time we are in our late teens, we have also begun to recognize that it is not only our inner "beauties" that we project onto others, but also our inner "uglies." The four-year-old child has heroines who represent to her the strengths and resources that lie within herself. But she also has "anti-heroines" who mirror back to her the faults and weaknesses which are latent in her own character.

It is important to bring back the example of the small child, because this highlights the fact that projection is at work long before self-awareness is developed. In itself, "projection" is a neutral mechanism. It is neither morally good nor morally bad. It is merely a word for describing a key psychological mechanism through which we find out about ourselves, beginning when we are very young. As we get older, we become more discerning about ourselves and other people, but projection is still alive and well and at work in us. For example, when reading a novel or watching a movie, we tend to favor the character whose Great Story is similar to our own. A novelist who is a Sage-Seeker made the observation that the heroes of his stories are invariably Sages and Seekers.

At Clare's party, an open house where few people knew one another, projection was going on in every direction. Mature or immature, you and I project. Maybe both of us are wonderfully unprejudiced people, but we both come to Clare's open house being who we are. We both know all the rhetoric having to do with openness to others. We both resist labeling or stereotyping other people. But I still have inchoate, unreflective, inarticulate, unnameable reactions to you when I first meet you. And so do you. Until we get a chance to know each other better, you and I are like all other people when they first meet: In spite of good intentions, we see each other through our projections.

There is nothing wrong or abnormal about this. Projection provides a kind of anchor, a familiar and solid place where I start from who I am and then try to relate to who you are. In adulthood as in childhood, projection can show us what lies latent within ourselves. It is often in our projections onto others that we come to new discoveries about ourselves. This is especially true of our negative projections, the projection onto others of the dark or undeveloped side of our personalities.

Carl Jung called this undeveloped side the *shadow*. This is a useful image which accurately describes how everything that is bright in us has its dark side as well. If I walk in the sun, I cast a shadow. If there were no substance to me, there would be no shadow. Psychologically, what the metaphor of the shadow suggests is simply this: If there is any substance to me, if I have any solid character about me, I necessarily cast a shadow. The shadow is the flip-side of my conscious personality, my conscious ego, the face I present to the world.

Not that the shadow is bad. There is nothing "bad" about the shadow I cast when I stand in the sun's light. But there is darkness in that spot, not sunlight. So it is with our psychological shadow. Let's say that I am an assertive sort of person, self-confident in my ways, used to taking the initiative in any project. When I meet people who don't manifest these qualities, I get impatient with them. To me they are wishy-washy. But in other people's eyes, they might be the salt of the earth. They are receptive, flexible, and understanding in all the ways that I am not. They even get things done in a way that I can't, because they are more sensitive and adaptable than I am.

Who is right and who is wrong? Who is more virtuous? The answer is: neither. I am likely to be annoyed by the person who appears wishy-washy to me. But that person is just as likely to be put off by my assertiveness, which he sees as rigid, insensitive, and aggressive. Both of us are projecting a "shadow." Both of us are picking up in the other person what is undeveloped in ourselves.

Both of us are projecting what we see as "uglies" in each other. But in fact both of us need a little of what the other has.

The shadow is at work in collective ways as well, and it plays an important role in all political conflicts. In the early 70's, on the highway from the airport to the city of Moscow, there was a series of billboards containing cartoons which depicted the Soviet soldier-worker, a rifle in one hand and a sickle in the other, standing victoriously on the neck of monsters and dragons who were Nazi soldiers on one billboard, and American soldiers in Vietnam on the next. American feelings about the Soviets don't usually appear so blatantly on billboards, but President Reagan's rhetoric about an "evil empire" is no less subtle. When the shadow is at work in political conflicts, one side tends to project *all* the evil, real or imagined, onto the other side.

This is precisely the trick which the shadow plays on us, collectively or individually. The evil, the fault, the weakness is always *outside* ourselves. The evil always lies elsewhere: in another person, another religion, another political system. The film "The Empire Strikes Back" gives us a dramatic illustration of the problem of the shadow. Darth Vader, who is all evil, is the shadow of Luke Skywalker, who is all good. In a fantasy sequence, Luke goes into the jungle to fight Vader. Luke kills Vader, and then lifts the forbidding black mask that has always hidden Vader's face. The face under the mask turns out to be Luke's own face.

This illustrates vividly how the shadow is a kind of *alter ego*, another person within ourselves who reflects what is dark or undeveloped in our bright and conscious personality. The function of the shadow is to represent the opposite side of our egos. In so doing, the shadow embodies those qualities that we tend to dislike most in other people, especially people of the same sex as ourselves.

The shadow is the flip-side of the conscious ego. So if I am a man, I project my shadow most readily onto other men. If I am a woman, I see my dark side most quickly in other women. Like every generalization, this one has exceptions. Husband and wife, for instance, pick up their shadows in each other. But the rule holds good as a general guide.

The shadow can consist of *shortcomings* or negative qualities which I pick up in someone else. These qualities might be real enough in the other person, but at the same time they are usually things that I need to overcome in myself. The shadow also has a bright side. In this case my shadow is activated by *positive* qualities in another person. But because these qualities are dark or undeveloped in *me*, I experience them in a negative way in someone else. This aspect of the shadow is illustrated in the "assertive" versus "sensitive" persons described above.

In both cases, dark or bright, my shadow is telling me to look at myself. Whether or not the person bearing my projection actually possesses the qualities I see in them, I have to discern whether my negative reaction involves (1) a shortcoming I should correct or (2) a life-giving quality I need to develop.

Let's return to Clare's open house. Many of the interactions that took place among the guests are explained by the concepts we have just been discussing. Recall what was said earlier: until two people come to know each other fairly well, they see each other through their projections. Projections of the *shadow* are the most common of all projections among people of the same sex. And my shadow is activated especially when I first meet a person who is living the Great Story that is opposite to my own.

Opposite archetypes of the same sex are initially threatening or antagonistic toward each other. This general principle helps to explain some of our basic reactions to other people.

Amy's reaction to Alexandra is typical. Here is the Mediatrix meeting the Amazon. Amy lets life happen. She is curious and fascinated by everything that unfolds around her. Although she has a mind of her own, she appears unfocused and passive. Alex on the other hand is the embodiment of all the direction, ambition, and action that Amy lacks. Alex immediately names the reason why she is put off by Amy. If she were to reflect further, she might discover that Amy has some qualities that are absent in herself. Alex is so goal-oriented that she dismisses the unexpected and misses the unknown.

Clare and Meg have known each other for years and are close friends. But when they first met in college, their reactions to each other were similar to those of Amy and Alex. Working together on a course project helped them to set aside their initial reactions and to appreciate the differences. They found that they complement each other, and through the years they have come to trust each other and count on each other's strengths. Meg is Mother, and her way of getting things done is a good balance to Clare's approach. Meg gets frustrated with Clare's thoughtless ways, but she knows that Clare is attentive and helpful to people in her own way.

A person who lives the Great Story opposite to our own has such different values and priorities from our own that we can feel "negated" in their presence. This is particularly true for someone who is young or immature, someone who has not yet owned either the strengths or the limitations inherent in his or her archetype. Amy and Alexandra are youthful versions of their respective archetypes. Each of them picks up in the other what is dark and unformed in herself. They are both hit with the full impact of each other's shadows, and that is why they appear threatening to each other.

Neither Amy nor Alex has much sense of any archetype other than her own. Alex is an Amazon whose way of being is well supported by today's society. She is thrilled by what she is doing in the real-estate business and she gets plenty of strokes. The Great Story opposite to her own, that of the Mediatrix, is so foreign to her that she doesn't recognize it as a legitimate way of being. To her Amy is aimless. Amy is equally threatened by Alex, but she doesn't get much affirmation from society for her attention to the unseen or for her idealism.

As a result, the two young women experience their "shadows" in different ways. Alex feels antagonism toward Amy. Amy feels insecure in the presence of Alex. These feelings apply to other archetypes than those of Amy and Alex, and they apply to men as well as to women. *Antagonism* and *insecurity* seem to be woven from the same cloth. Different as they might appear, both of these feelings are typical reactions to an encounter with our shadow.

Alex is exuberant, and these are her times. Amy is not the only woman who feels intimidated by Alex and what she represents. Meg is Mother and Clare is Companion. Both are independent and responsible women who have interesting careers, but they feel more fulfilled and are more themselves when mothering and companioning. Meg and Clare are typical of many women today who hold good jobs and feel a sense of accomplishment. They don't like the insinuation that you can't have a full life until every moment of the day is filled with coordinated activity. Women who are not Amazons are overwhelmed by the choices and expectations presented today in every popular women's magazine. Women who are not Amazons can be exhausted just by leafing through and reading the titles of the articles.

Our general principle states that opposite archetypes of the same sex *initially* experience a sense of antagonism toward each other. The word *initially* is important. Meg and Clare have opposite stories, but they know each other well and have long since overcome the effects of the shadow in their relationship. Not that the shadow disappears. One's shadow is invariably activated in the presence of one's opposite archetype. A person who is living the story opposite to our own is always an incarnate reminder to us of the qualities that are "shadiest" in ourselves. But as we mature, we no longer *act on* our shadow projections. We discern the difference between the real person and our projections, and we come to appreciate the qualities that are bright and life-giving in them.

This is true for Fred. He is a mature Father who no longer feels antagonistic toward Seekers like Randy, even when they are as immature as Randy seems to be. Fred is a widower with a son of his own. Meeting men like Randy makes him wish that he had allowed his son to travel as he wanted to before he went to college. At the age of 55, Fred securely possesses his own Father-story, and he is well aware that there are other archetypes, other ways of being which are as legitimate as his own.

Randy is a Seeker-Sage, and at the party he casts his shadow more on Warren than on Fred. His shadow is activated from the direction of his second or auxiliary archetype, and his inner Sage is put off by Warren's aggressive Warrior talk. To Warren, Randy is typical of many men he meets in his line of business who refuse to grow up. Warren is a self-confident businessman who does not want to rub people the wrong way. As a salesman he has learned to put on a good front, and he tries not to let his shadow show. But there is a lot of annoyance and anger bottled up in Warren.

Theoretically, according to our rule of thumb, Warren should feel initially threatened by Sloane, who is his opposite. Sometimes Warren does feel insecure in the presence of Sages who have a breadth of understanding that he knows he lacks. But he finds silly Sages like Sloane to be windbags. As for Sloane, he is so full of himself that he doesn't realize the effect he has on other people. Alone at night, Sloane wonders why with all of his cleverness he has no friends. Basically he is jealous of people like Warren, but he hides his jealousy (and his lack of accomplishment) beneath the veneer of big words and high-sounding ideas.

We have been talking about opposite archetypes of the same sex. Archetypes of the opposite sex affect each other quite differently. *Opposite archetypes of the opposite sex are initially fasci-*

nating to each other. Fascinating, not threatening. Intriguing, not menacing.

Fred and Clare are Father and Companion, opposite archetypes of the opposite sex. Their attraction to each other involves quite a different kind of projection from that of the shadow. Fred and Clare met only a short time ago. The mechanism of projection is still very much at work in the way they perceive each other, and it will continue to be strongly at work until they pass through the initial stages of their attraction. Clare, who has gone through many relationships with men, knows well the sensation of fascination. She has dated many Fathers, some younger than herself, and she has always been intrigued by their common-sense values and their need to look after her. This time, with Fred, she seems ready to persist beyond the stage of being fascinated by values that are so different from her own free-wheeling ways.

Fred has been settled in his Fatherly ways from the time he was a child. He is a widower whose first wife was a Mother. Like many Fathers and Mothers, Fred and his wife found each other when they were young adults, they married, they raised a son, and they were happy. His wife's death was a blow to him, and it was several years before he wanted to get out and meet other women. Fred is intrigued with Clare, who is so different from his first wife. He is aware that the difference accounts for much of the attraction, and so he is cautious. As of December 27 and Clare's party, Fred is wondering if a long-term relationship is possible. Fred would like this, but he knows they will both have to come to terms with different priorities, different values, and the different ways of seeing life that belong to Father and Companion.

Warren and Amy represent a different set of opposite archetypes—Warrior and Mediatrix. They met for the first time at Clare's party, and their reactions to each other illustrate another way in which opposite archetypes of the opposite sex are initially fascinating to each other. Amy is a fey spirit, a Mediatrix-Companion. (Recall that the Mediatrix strongly needs the help of a second archetype, either Companion or Mother, in order to anchor herself in the real world.) Amy was delighted when Warren came over to chat with her. She has had many spontaneous relationships with Eternal Boys like Randy, whom she just met on the plane. The Randys of this world are natural "soul companions" to her and she is always likely to stumble onto Randy. What really intrigues her is men like Warren who know what they want and go after it.

Interestingly enough, Amy is *fascinated* by the same qualities in Warren that *antagonize* her when she sees them in Alexandra. Opposite archetypes of the opposite sex react quite differently from opposite archetypes of the same sex.

Warren has the same sort of experience in his attraction to Amy. Objectively, the Mediatrix seems to contradict everything the Warrior stands for. But this is not how the Mediatrix looks, initially, to the Warrior. Warren is fascinated by Amy's mediumistic qualities, and he is determined to talk to her before the party is over. Sloane, the Sage without wisdom, exhibits many of Amy's vague qualities. To Warren, Sloane is simply an idealistic windbag. Amy is a young Mediatrix, not any better focused than Sloane. But Warren finds in her a kind of "ethereal depth."

Why the fascination between opposites of the opposite sex, when opposites of the same sex bring out one's shadow?

In both cases we are dealing with projections, especially the *initial* projections that are made when two people meet. Let us go back to the basic description of this psychological mechanism: Projection has to do with the fact that we do not first experience our own inner qualities within ourselves. We first see those qualities in other people, who mirror back to us the qualities that lie within ourselves.

The shadow is the flip-side of the conscious ego, and any person's *conscious ego* contains a gender, male or female. If I am a man, the person on whom I project my shadow mirrors back to me the qualities that are dark or undeveloped in me *as a man*. If I am a woman, the person on whom I project my shadow reflects back to me the qualities that are shadiest in my conscious ego, my conscious personality *as a woman*. Man or woman, when I am faced with my shadow, I am inclined to experience it negatively— with feelings of antagonism or insecurity, for instance—because the shadow makes me aware of the dark side of the personality that I present to the world. The shadow is menacing, and people of the opposite archetype and the same sex as myself can be menacing, because they challenge the values that I consciously live as a man or as a woman.

Projections onto persons of the opposite sex are different. Every woman has within herself an "inner masculine," that is, qualities which men live out quite naturally in their conscious personalities but which a woman absorbs only with effort, usually in the second half of life. The same is true for a man and his "inner feminine." It is these components of the psyche that seem to be activated, strongly but unconsciously, when we meet someone of the opposite sex who lives the Great Story that is totally different from our own. We will return to these concepts of masculine and feminine in Chapter 9.

We wear our archetypes like a suit of clothing. We project our Great Story to others very quickly, often before we have said a word. This is most likely to be true of people who live their archetype in an unconscious way. In this case the archetype shows up blatantly, especially the dark side, and we experience a stereotype more than a real person. But for everyone, no matter how mature we are, our archetype is often the first word we speak. It is like an aura. Invisible to ourselves, it picks up the unconscious projections of others. This is neither good nor bad, just a neutral fact. The best thing we can do about it is to become more aware of our Great Story and to recognize both its virtues and its limitations. Then we are less likely to become walking stereotypes.

"It takes one to know one." Mother recognizes Mother, and

a Seeker readily identifies a fellow Seeker. A Sage quickly spots a pseudo-Sage, who might be a Warrior pretending to be what he is not. A Mediatrix can tell the difference between a true mediumistic woman and an intuitive Amazon. The reverse is also true. The Amazon has difficulty being supportive of a Mediatrix who is trying to wear an Amazon veneer in order to cope in the marketplace.

Understanding our own story and appreciating the other Great Stories helps us to relate to other people with confidence. Despite good intentions, communication breaks down and we don't know why. Archetypal differences help to explain this problem. Recognizing our Great Story enables us to become more independent. We can free ourselves from the mystique of others, from the hold that others can have on us even without intending it, and we can recognize the ways in which we have given other people power over us. As I mature in my own archetype, appreciation and admiration come to replace anxiety and annoyance in my encounters with others.

8

MARRIAGE · MIDLIFE

In one of Ruth Rendell's detective stories, Inspector Wexford is investigating a murder that involves an elderly couple who had been married for forty years. It was the wife who was murdered, and the husband is a suspect. Wexford is talking to Irene Bell, who had known the Knightons for many years.

"Was it a happy marriage, Miss Bell?"

"Someone said that the state of marriage is unhappy only insofar as life itself is unhappy."

"Samuel Johnson said it. What do you say?"

"In general, Mr. Wexford, I don't think much of it. It goes on too long. If it could be for five years, say, I think it would be an excellent institution. Who can stand the same person morning, noon and night for forty years? People think a single woman of my age hasn't married because she hasn't had a chance. That's not so of course. . . . I'm not much to look at and never have been but neither are most of the married women you see around you. If folks only got married because they were pretty or charming it'd be a world of singles. No, I never fancied marriage myself. I don't much like sharing. I don't like cooking or housework or babies or sex. Oh, yes, I've tried sex. I tried it three times forty years ago and those three times were enough for a lifetime in my opinion. But those are my views. That's marriage in general. In particular, which is what you're asking, I daresay the Knightons were as happy as most people."[1]

Miss Bell would probably not make a successful marriage counselor, but her opinions about marriage contain some worthwhile points. When is a marriage "happy"? Inspector Wexford was asking a difficult question. Irene Bell's answer is realistic. A marriage that has lasted is not necessarily romantic, exciting, stimulating, or even a good union. All we know is that it has lasted. In the next few pages, we will make some generalizations about "happy" marriages. The adjective should be understood with Miss Bell's cautions in mind.

Our first generalization is this, and it is based on personal stories that hundreds of people have shared with us: *Most happily married people have complementary archetypes.* This is the situation where Father is married to Mother, Seeker to Companion, Warrior to Amazon, and Sage to Mediatrix. The archetypes here do not have to be a person's dominant archetype. The similarity can take place through the auxiliary archetype, for instance, when Mother-Amazon is married to Seeker-Warrior. In this example the couple finds their communality in their secondary archetypes, in this case Amazon and Warrior.

We should add that the same thing applies to friendships between two people of the same sex. Often it is the auxiliary archetype that explains the close bond between two men or two women whose stories and values are very different because of opposing dominant archetypes. A Seeker-Sage described his relationship with a Father-Sage in these words: "We are hopelessly friends."

Complementary archetypes enable many couples to rise above the differences that are often destructive in a marriage, such as a wide difference in age or in cultural background. Another kind of difference, usually less apparent to outsiders, is a radical dissimilarity in personal stories, as when an only child marries the eldest of ten. When a couple shares similar archetypes, they have similar priorities and basic values which go a long way to overcome the kind of differences that lead to marriage break-up.

It is not impossible for *opposite* archetypes to have a successful marriage. But if the marriage is a happy one, the partners were aware of their differences and accepted them as complementary before they made a permanent commitment. In the case of opposite archetypes what often happens—and it is disastrous—is that one partner expects the other to adapt, or to change with time. A Mother who marries a Seeker is doomed to failure if she expects to change his Seeker's ways. It is for a similar reason that Fred is not ready to rush into a marriage with Clare. He is not yet certain of all the implications of her Companion nature, and he is wise enough to know that Clare will never see "settling down" the way he sees it. For her part, Clare will never be able to expect from Fred the same kind of adventure or excitement she gets from some of her friends who are not Fathers.

Marriages between opposites can be compatible or comfortable enough, but they are not always life-giving or growth-producing. If both partners live out of opposite stories and do not develop an auxiliary archetype, as time goes on they are likely to exhibit more and more of the immature side of their archetype.

Dan and Janet are both 47. They have been married for twenty-four years and for most of that time have lived in a small southeastern city. Dan has recently received his Ph.D. and is head of Counseling Services in a large high school. Janet teaches home economics at the local junior high. They are childless—a bitter disappointment for Janet and a great relief for Dan.

They met in college when both volunteered to work on a blood drive. Dan was immediately intrigued by the way Janet took charge. He was impressed by the way she delegated duties without being condescending. She was able to call forth the best efforts from her fellow students and get the job done efficiently. This was quite a contrast to the way Dan worked. He was never very directive and always preferred working alongside others, playing things by ear.

Janet was attracted by Dan's Eternal-Boy qualities, his adaptability, his easy and ready acceptance of others. Dan's optimism and his indifference to status were endearing to her. They became romantically involved but did not marry until they had both graduated. By that time they had recognized their basic differences, which they did not see as disruptive. Dan introduced Janet to new people and new ideas, while Janet mentored and mothered Dan.

Dan is Seeker-Sage, Janet is Mother-Amazon. Both are aware of their strengths, both are capable in their jobs. But in their marriage, as the years have gone on, both have neglected their opposites. Each compensates for what the other lacks instead of encouraging the other to be more self-sufficient. What was once a compatible relationship has become a sad joke to those who know them well.

On Friday night Dan comes home from work, enters by the back door and shouts, "Mother, I'm home!" Janet responds with "Wipe your feet, Danny." Dan asks if he can bring his dog in, a mangy German Shepherd. Janet replies, "Yes, if you take him right downstairs to your room." Dan takes Rex downstairs to his den where he relaxes, watches some TV, and cleans his fish tanks. In a while Janet calls down and tells him his supper is ready.

Over dinner Dan discusses his students and some of the difficulties they are having. Janet tells Dan about the state of their checking account and informs him of holiday arrangements she has made with their travel agent. As he reaches for a second pork chop Janet expresses concern over his cholesterol intake, and she reminds him to take out the garbage after dinner.

The doorbell rings. Dan's buddies are off to a ball game and stop by to see if he can come along. Dan returns to the kitchen and asks, "Mother, can I have my allowance for the weekend?" Janet gives him some money and reminds him that it has to last for the whole week. Dan goes off to the game. Janet clears the table and does the dishes.

Dan and Janet are in fact happy in their marriage. Their trade-off of deficiencies is not obvious to them, though it is to everyone else. This is a case where compatibility has become complacency, and stereotype becomes caricature.

The story of Dan and Janet sounds so far-fetched that some

readers may think it is exaggerated fiction. It is not. Dan and Janet are extreme examples of opposite archetypes in a marriage. There are less blatant examples which are more familiar to most of us.

She was the bouncy blonde cheerleader. He was the football hero. Together they were the ideal couple in the class of '51. Paul and Melanie married the summer they graduated from high school. He called her "his princess," and he was her knight in shining armor. They were admired and envied by all. Melanie worked at the corner drugstore while Paul attended college for two years before joining the police force.

They had two children when they were in their early twenties. Paul worked shifts, and Melanie was grateful for the children's company. The children soon adjusted to her all-or-nothing form of parenting. When Paul was working, Melanie spent hours making papier-mâché creatures with her children. She took them to the movies or to visit her friends. Mealtimes with Melanie were fun and intimate, and the children felt important and cherished. When Paul was home, however, he was the center of their mother's attention, and they felt left out and pushed into the background.

Paul is a Warrior-Father who found Melanie's companioning ways flattering. He took pride in protecting her from the practical realities of earning an income, making decisions and being responsible for herself. Gradually his opinions became her opinions, and she ate when he was hungry. She always wore blue, his favorite color. After two driving lessons she gave up, conceding that it was easier to take the bus or to let Paul do the driving.

When the children got older, Melanie thought about taking some college courses. Paul did not support this idea. She proposed working a few days a week at Sears. Paul discouraged her. He didn't want his princess working, and besides they didn't need the money. Now in her fifties, Melanie spends her time attending craft classes and shopping. She always makes a point of getting home before Paul returns from work.

Paul and Melanie's marriage is compatible and comfortable. She needs him, and he needs her to be there for him. But in the last analysis, each counts on the other to remain undeveloped and dependent.

We have alluded in earlier chapters to the changes or transitions that take place in midlife. It is often in midlife that people feel the call to develop a second archetype. But maturity does not demand that everyone must enter into another Great Story. Some people find fulfillment throughout their lives in a single archetype. As their lives unfold they develop different facets of their one story, expanding it to meet new situations. This is especially true for the Mother or Father who in midlife finds new outlets for his or her Great Story—in the grandchildren perhaps, or in nurturing activities that take him or her into the larger community. (The Father or Mother who has never been married will probably have explored an auxiliary archetype before midlife.)

Midlife is defined in different ways. Chronologically, midlife has to do with the years between 35 and 50. This is a period during which everyone seems to experience some kind of change, radical or gradual, having to do with one's personal identity and attitude toward life. Current literature on midlife tends to emphasize that the "midlife crisis" has to do not so much with our age as with our relative maturity, how we have dealt with the psychological tasks that belong to each stage of life. For most of us, there is unresolved business from youth and childhood that has to be settled before a mature self-understanding is possible.

Talking about a second Great Story is a luxury for some people. The crisis of midlife often involves accepting one's *first and dominant* archetype, after years of trying to escape from it.

Anne has spent most of her life trying to deny the Mother archetype which she knows is her dominant story. Her own mother was an immature woman who fluctuated between being a smothering Mother and a martyr-Mother. In reaction, Anne made a conscious effort to ignore her own nurturing instincts. She decided to remain single and to pursue a career. She did not want to affect any children of her own the way her mother had plagued her.

Imitating her Amazon sister, Anne worked at being objective and purposeful. Despite all her efforts to be impersonal, she constantly perceived and dealt with the office staff as though it was an extended family. It was Anne who began the custom of remembering everyone's birthdays and anniversaries, and it was she who decorated the office for every imaginable holiday. At times her thoughtfulness disrupted the efficiency of the office and became something of a nuisance. Not surprisingly, when Anne was given a position of authority, the staff experienced her as a matriarch.

At 39, Anne is tired and frustrated. Too long she has been trying to live the Amazon story, which is not hers. She has not been doing this very successfully. In trying to deny her dominant story which is Mother, she has for the most part been living the darker and "smothering" aspects of Mother. Anne is resentful of the Amazon businesswomen who have climbed higher than she has, and at the same time she is envious of women who have had children. She is now becoming aware of the problem she has created for herself by over-reacting to her mother's style of parenting.

Many Seekers find themselves in Anne's situation, trying to own their original story later in life. We have mentioned that the Seeker archetype does not get nearly the support from society that Father and Warrior do. Seekers take many detours on their journey before they settle into a profession or a relationship, and they rarely end up doing exactly what they set out to do in the beginning. Because it takes them longer to focus, Seekers constantly hear that they are "going through a stage." Or, especially if there are no other Seekers in the family, they are led to believe they are potential "black sheep" (an image which one would never apply to a Father, however immature). Lack of support from family and community prevents many Seekers from owning their archetype as early as they might.

Before we talk about the development of a second archetype, it might be useful to repeat the diagram:

	MOTHER		FATHER	
AMAZON		MEDIATRIX	WARRIOR		SAGE
	COMPANION		SEEKER	

Recall that Mother-Companion and Father-Seeker, the archetypes printed vertically, have to do with our ways of relating *personally*. The contrasts among these archetypes involve differences in the way we relate to other people. Amazon-Mediatrix and Warrior-Sage, printed horizontally in the diagram, are archetypes that deal with the *non-personal* world of accomplishment, power, ideas, knowledge, insight, hunch, wisdom, and other objective and a-personal realities.

These concepts indicate why a second archetype provides an important balance. A second archetype helps keep our dominant story from becoming exaggerated. Anyone whose dominant archetype is personal needs a good way to connect with the non-personal world. Companions and Seekers, for example, are often "stabilized" through their auxiliary archetype which offers them objectivity and complements their free-wheeling ways. Conversely, people whose dominant archetype is non-personal are often "humanized" by their auxiliary story, which is one of the personal archetypes. Many a Sage who is wrapped up in his world of ideas and theories avoids becoming odd because his auxiliary archetype, Father or Seeker, helps him to connect with real people. One Amazon, a New York advertising executive, stated her need for a second archetype in this way: "I woke up one morning realizing that I had spent fifteen years loving work, but hadn't put any work into loving."

As we mentioned in Chapter 4, many people find identity and fulfillment in *two* archetypes throughout their lives. They live two of the Great Stories pretty much simultaneously, and they achieve maturity with the aid of two archetypes. One archetype governs their relationships with people while the other connects them with the non-personal world. This is not an uncommon pattern. For some people, however, it is not until the second half of life that a second archetype emerges. For sake of a shorthand term, let's call this the *archetypal shift*.

When it takes place in midlife, an archetypal shift can be unsettling and confusing. It has a profound effect on marriages and other close relationships, because two people rarely move into a second Great Story at exactly the same time. One says to the other "You're different from the man I used to know" or "You aren't the woman I married." The observation is often quite correct, because the other person has begun to live a different story.

But an archetypal shift does not happen overnight. The change is obviously confusing to the spouse or friend who is observing it. It is equally confusing to the person who is undergoing it and who does not understand exactly what is happening. The job that used to be challenging, the activities that used to be exciting, are all suddenly boring and unfulfilling. The problem with an archetypal shift is that while one's dominant story is waning, the second story has not yet come into focus. This takes time, and the intervening period can be filled with depression and a sense that one's world has fallen apart.

Colin was a well-established corporation lawyer when he married Natalie. Like many Fathers he had postponed marriage until he was in position to provide comfortably for his future family. Natalie was an archetypal Mother teaching elementary school and biding her time until a Father came along. Teaching young children had confirmed her in her longing for a family of her own. Colin and Natalie had four children, and they both thrived on parenting. Most of their leisure time was filled with camping, drive-in movies, hockey games, and other family outings. Given their common goals and shared values, both Colin and Natalie thought that their marriage was close to being ideal.

At age 37 Natalie was surprised to find that she wanted more time alone and less time with the family. The children were getting older and were doing more things on their own. Colin was the only one who was disappointed when Natalie stopped going to hockey games with them.

Natalie began to lose interest in all the homemaking activities that she once found enjoyable and creative. She started to feel depressed for no reason she could name. This was disturbing for Colin, who counted on her being in good spirits when he came home from the office. Usually an enthusiastic and energetic person, now she was lethargic. Bewildered and confused, she began sleeping later each morning. Natalie rarely had wine with a meal, but now she found herself pouring a drink early in the day and settling down for an afternoon of TV. She used to enjoy cooking, and many evening meals were gourmet events. Now she opened cans and packages at the last minute.

Colin suggested that perhaps Natalie had outgrown motherhood and should return to teaching. But the thought of another face under 14 made her cringe. Natalie felt used and useless. Over the next few years she would find herself standing in the living room crying. It was as though she was mourning the past, with no future to look forward to. She wanted to run away but there was no place to go.

Colin wanted to be understanding, but he couldn't fathom Natalie's discontent when she had everything she had always wanted. He encouraged her to read instead of wasting her time with TV. They went out to dinner alone and took long walks together. Natalie wasn't good company, but gradually her concentration returned and with it a sense of purpose. Instead of returning to teaching she decided to explore other possibilities.

Natalie was not alone in her depression. Colin often wasn't

better company to her than she was to him. He was disliking the pressures of his law practice. He was weary of the long days and the many evenings he had to devote to his work in order to keep on top of things. For the first time in his life he was feeling tired and vulnerable. His children noticed that he was chronically irritable. Colin liked his profession but knew that he needed a change. After a year of thinking things through, he decided to give up his private practice. At a drastic cut in salary, he took a teaching position at the university law school. This was a difficult decision for Colin. He had always prided himself on the way he had provided for his family, and the reduction in his income would inevitably change their lifestyle.

The year after Colin began his teaching job, Natalie opened a shop that specializes in educational toys for children. Natalie's second archetype, Amazon, is giving her a sense of freedom and a feeling of self-worth that is new to her. Colin is very supportive. Natalie has benefited from his sound legal advice and knowledge of business. As for Colin, he has found in his new position a good environment in which he can pass on his knowledge and experience to others. Free from the pressures of business, he has time for the study and research he had always wanted to do. His second archetype, Sage, has set him on a new course in the second half of life.

Natalie and Colin in their mid-forties have not abandoned their Mother and Father archetypes. These are still their personal ways of relating. But they are now finding new identity and fulfillment in second archetypes, Amazon and Sage. These happen to be opposite archetypes, and in their case this has been beneficial. As Mother and Father, Natalie and Colin almost took each other for granted. As Amazon and Sage, they are quite intrigued with each other, and each is proud of the other's endeavors. Living opposite stories is not a problem for them. Their marital problems came during the time of transition when the new archetypes were emerging but hadn't yet found an outlet.

Colin and Natalie's children have not suffered from the change. They had been getting older, and they were finding that all the family "togetherness" encouraged by their parents was getting to be a bore and a burden. Their parents' new lifestyle has made the children more independent and responsible.

Statistics tell us that many apparently stable marriages break down after fifteen years. *Archetypal shift* explains one of the reasons why. Couples who once had everything in common suddenly have nothing in common at all. "You aren't the person I married" and that's the end of it.

Colin and Natalie are fortunate. They married on the basis of complementary archetypes (Father and Mother) and now they are freshly fascinated with each other as their auxiliary archetypes have emerged. Archetypal shift could have ended their marriage, but as it turns out they have become intrigued with each other for the first time in their lives. This can also happen for couples with opposite archetypes who married on the basis of an initial attraction which wore off quickly. In midlife, with the emergence of auxiliary archetypes, they now have something in common and in the second half of life they have a more stable marriage than they had in the first.

Opposite archetypes, of course, can affect relationships other than marriages. In any relationship where you and the other person live opposite stories, it will often seem that the harder you try to be understanding, and the more activities you share in the name of togetherness, the more frustrated you become. One week you will blame the other for being selfish and thoughtless, and the next week you feel it's your fault for appearing demanding in being attentive to your own needs. If two people have opposite archetypes and live their archetypes unconsciously, they can become discouraged, exhausted, and bitter when they do not know the reasons for the constant conflict of interests.

In midlife there is a sense of time running out. So much left to do and so little time in which to do it—a crisis of limits. Some single men and women, including members of celibate communities, for the first time feel drawn to marriage and hope for children of their own. At the same time many who have been married for years leave their marriage and children to search for identity as a single person. However, some men and women change vocations or professions prematurely, thinking that a change of scene will ease the pain and confusion of the midlife transition.

The 45-year-old Seeker who married in his twenties and has raised a family now feels restless and confined. (Of course men of all archetypes, not just Seekers, can experience the same thing.) Our Seeker leaves his wife and family. After a year of freedom he begins looking for companionship. He soon gets involved with an attractive young Mother, whom he mistakes for a Companion. Within a short time he finds himself starting a second family— just the opposite from his original intention.

Many singles panic when they are faced with the reality of advancing years. They decide to spend the rest of their lives with someone whom they wouldn't have spent a weekend with ten years earlier.

Sometimes midlife begins with the symptoms described in the story of Colin and Natalie: inner realities call us to renew life. Other times midlife is thrust on us by outer events: a divorce, an illness, the death of a friend who is our own age, a car accident, the loss of a job. For some the outer crisis calls forth a hidden strength. Her husband dies, and the once dependent wife learns to drive, balances the bank account, and retrains for future employment. She misses her husband but discovers herself to be an independent and capable person.

On the other hand, for many the midlife crisis reveals a deficiency. There is a divorce, and the man who was always in control, strong and confident and self-sufficient, suddenly feels lost.

His vulnerability is a new experience for him, and he sees his vulnerability as a weakness. Without taking time to grieve and to reorient himself, he marries within eighteen months.

Many angry, aggressive Amazons are in fact Companions or Mothers whose Amazon story is emerging in the second half of life. Before this second archetype comes fully into focus for them, they go through a tumultuous time during which they feel they have been "had" by men, by children, by life in general.

Many Mothers and Fathers have denied their own desires and needs in the name of nurturing and protecting others. In midlife what Mother or Father wants is perhaps time alone, or a luxury purchase, or time to develop a skill or pursue a hobby that has no other purpose than personal fulfillment. If they haven't entered into themselves and recognized what they very legitimately want for *themselves*, Mother or Father will become resentful, and the resentment will erupt in many forms during midlife. Overly devoted Mothers and Fathers, like overly committed Amazons and Warriors, are prime candidates for midlife burnout.

The young Companion who is afraid of becoming dependent sometimes tries to act like an Amazon. So does the young Mother who feels guilty about spending her time in nurturing activities. In the end these women do not fully own or develop either archetype. The transition to the second story (in this case Amazon) is more peaceful if one does not somehow oblige herself to deny the first story in order to explore the second one.

How our parents lived out their Great Stories has a lasting effect on us. Usually midlife makes it clear just what this effect is. For example, sons whose mothers were weak Companions or domineering Mothers have missed out on some essential nurturing. This affects their relationships with all other women. Some sons become resentful and abusive, seeking power over women. Others constantly seek the care and attention which they didn't receive as children. These men are usually looking for the ideal Mother. When asked to describe such a woman, they list qualities from all four of the feminine archetypes. The problem is that no such woman exists, and so their search goes on.

Daughters who were parented by authoritarian Fathers or selfish Seekers often remain immature in their relationships with other men. They lack the inner confidence fostered by a loving father, and it takes them a long time to become their own selves. Some daughters remain little girls all their lives; they are caught in a time warp where they are forever waiting for Daddy. Other women appear to be self-confident and mature, but inwardly they long for the appreciation and attention of Father. They may appear aloof or independent, wanting to prove to themselves and others that they don't miss the support and affirmation which they were never given. Not surprisingly, the father whom these daughters long for is a composite of all four masculine archetypes. Like the ideal Mother, he does not exist. Sons who have not been affirmed by their female parent and daughters who have not been affirmed by their male parent—no matter what archetypes are involved—develop an insatiable thirst for attention and affirmation.

Maturity requires us to be realistic about our parents as people. Often enough, we do not begin developing this realism until midlife, precisely because it is not until midlife that we begin to get realistic about ourselves. We will perpetuate the pains of childhood if we continue to idealize and project upon our parents. *Midlife is a time for naming, not blaming.*

We need to be patient with ourselves and others during the midlife transition. It is not a time of "crisis" for everyone, but it is certainly a time when everyone experiences boundaries and limitations. This experience, as psychologist James R. Zullo suggests, is an experience of new beginnings:

> Knowing my limits frees me from being something I am not. Being aware of my boundaries allows me to experiment and test new possibilities and options. I learn to maximize the use of my time; because I have less time I work more selectively

and intelligently. . . . Although the crisis of limits is an in-
voluntary process, I can decide how I am going to interpret its
meaning and respond to its invitations and challenges. . . . It
is an invitation to "grow down" into life, a time to discover and
make friends with the person I truly am. The crisis of limits is
essentially a reorientation to the truth about myself and my
world.[2]

Reverend Jim Jones, the leader of the People's Temple who
founded Jonestown in the jungle of Guyana, offers us a tragic example of someone who could not face the truth about himself and
his world. He was a Seeker who drifted from one church to another before he established his own, changing his message as new
ideas moved him. He was a Warrior who fought for one liberal
cause after another, engaging leading politicians in his cam-
paigns. Establishing himself as the only source of law and guid-
ance and even sex in his community, Jones insisted that his
followers call him Father, and he issued his disciplinary edicts
from a throne. A self-proclaimed Sage, he was in fact a charlatan
who ordered his followers to buy, and sell to the public, small
pictures of himself to ward off evil. In his forties, near the end of
his life, he started calling himself God. Jim Jones' last act was to
impose suicide on himself and some nine hundred members of
his People's Temple in November of 1978.

Only people who are not rooted in a Great Story of their own
would hand their lives over to such a person. The irony is that Jim
Jones himself had no roots in any archetype. He tried to be all
things to everyone. As a result he had no psychic center of his own
and was unable to "grow down" into life.

Knowing your Great Story is a significant way of discovering
who you are and who you are not.

Notes

1. Ruth Rendell, *The Speaker of Mandarin* (Arrow, 1983), pp 113–114.
2. James R. Zullo, "The Crisis of Limits: Midlife Beginnings," *Human Development*, 3 (Spring 1982) 7–8.

9

MATURITY

The leader of a symphony orchestra, interviewed during the intermission of a concert, said "I knew from the time I was nine years old that I was a conductor. I didn't choose it. It chose me." The sense of destiny expressed in this statement is even more true of archetypes than of any profession. No one sits down and decides which of the Great Stories he or she is going to live. No one chooses his or her archetype. The archetypes choose us.

Every religious tradition recognizes this reality. In Christian terms the archetypes are "calls" or "vocations." They are gifts of the Spirit of God that are far more basic to life than any of the specific vocational choices we make when we leave home. The work of developing and integrating one's archetype is at once a response to grace and a cooperation with grace. Some religions speak of "fate" rather than a divine "call" which a person answers. Whatever interpretation of life one may choose, fate or call, perennial wisdom recognizes the fact that there is a fundamental *givenness* about the story we live.

Heredity and environment do not explain the phenomenon we are dealing with here. The archetypes represented in any one family may be similar or they may be widely varied. A family can support one's archetype or on the other hand repress it. A supportive environment makes for a healthy self-image and a confident possession of one's archetype early in life. A family environment which gives little or no support to a person's archetype can lead to delayed development, depression, psychosis and even suicide. A person's family can have a powerful effect on the *development* of his or her archetype. But the family into which we are born does not genetically determine our archetype. In our experience with several thousand people, we have not been able to detect any pattern of inheritance. Theories about heredity and environment account for some important aspects of human behavior, but they do not take account of the basic *psychic orientation* represented in the archetypes.

Any psychological theory is a kind of *matrix* or *template* laid over human experience with the purpose of interpreting and naming and understanding our experience. No theory, no matrix provides answers to ultimate questions like "Why am I a Mother and not a Companion?" or "Where do the archetypes come from?" The great religions speak of a divine call, or fate, or a gift of God, and in this way they attempt to pick up where psychological methodology must leave off. Psychologically, all we can do is pick and choose among templates, lay each one over life and human experience, and decide which ones are most helpful and useful for interpreting our experience.

The Great Stories are one such template or matrix. The theory of archetypes presented in this book attempts to name patterns of psychic energy which are rooted in the collective history of humankind. These patterns are made actual and real in the personal stories of men and women in every era and every culture. This does not imply any philosophical determinism that would cripple one's essential freedom. Archetypes are inborn orientations that call forth our freedom and enlist it in the cause of active self-determination. Our free will is never more fully engaged than when we choose to *cooperate* with the archetypal trend that underlies our lives. It is this cooperation that leads to maturity and wholeness. In Christian terms, this is the cooperation with divine grace that leads to holiness.

We have already looked at many of the characteristics of maturity in each archetype. By way of summary, here are brief cameos that describe the archetypes as they appear when they have been well developed and consciously integrated:

FATHER discriminates between his instinct to provide or protect and the need that others actually have for his care and protection. He guards against imposing his sense of duty and discipline on others. He is not an absolute ruler, nor is he a benevolent dictator.

MOTHER acknowledges her own needs, abilities, and limitations. She recognizes whom she nurtures and why, and discerns how best to support those she cares for. She becomes more curious and less critical. She is not a devourer who feeds on the lives of those in her care.

SEEKER recognizes boundaries. He understands the difference between the adventure of the search and the search itself. He does not squander his energies on action for the sake of activity, or on activity for the sake of adventure. He is not an irresponsible drifter or a Peter Pan.

COMPANION discriminates between the experience of relating and the experience of caring. She is aware of the implications of her way of relating, and she becomes more compassionate and less passionate. She acknowledges what belongs to the relationship and what does not. She is not promiscuous, nor is she a dependent clinger.

WARRIOR is not governed by a need to conquer nor by his drive to succeed. He recognizes that there are forms of achievement and ways of succeeding that differ from his own. He is less concerned with productivity and efficiency, and more attentive to relationships and personal values. He is not a power-monger.

AMAZON does not compete for the sake of competing. She is more discerning when setting goals. Her instinct to achieve is balanced by an appreciation for the wisdom, values, and feelings of others. She is not an aggressive androgyne.

SAGE realizes the difference between knowledge and wisdom. He respects the experiences of others, and he makes his wisdom available to others in an uncondescending way. He is not an irrelevant theorizer, nor is he a charlatan.

MEDIATRIX is more focused and less vague. She recognizes her relationship with the collective unconscious and neither denies nor exaggerates it. She involves herself in activities that are a realistic expression of mediation. She is not a witch.

Maturity involves the *integration of opposites* within ourselves. Most adults have put effort into becoming rational, productive, independent, successful, however they may understand these goals. But mature adults have had to integrate the rational with all of the non-rational aspects of life. Productivity has to be integrated with leisure and simply "letting be." Independence has to be integrated with our dependence on others and our interrelatedness with others. Failure has to be assimilated along with success. These are the tasks of life that belong to everyone. However, the way I understand failure or success or independence or productivity comes from my Great Story, which may be different from yours. "Integration of opposites" takes a different shape for each person, a shape that the above cameos try to describe in capsule form.

Integration of opposites is the task of the second half of life. During the first half of life, we are testing out and living on what Roger Gould calls a major false assumption. We assume that there are "no significant opposite or contradictory forces within ourselves." We experience this major assumption through a variety of basic attitudes or minor false assumptions which dominate the first half of our lives:

Life appears to be simple and controllable.

Rewards will come automatically if we do what we're supposed to do.

There is only one right way to do things.

Commitment and effort will prevail over all other forces.

I am not like my parents in ways I don't want to be.

I am convinced that I can see the reality of those who are close to me quite clearly. [1]

Some of the assumptions of the first half of life are named in a more humorous vein by Ashleigh Brilliant in his collections of Brilliant Thoughts:

All I ask of life is a constant and exaggerated sense of my own importance.

I have just discovered the truth and can't understand why everyone isn't eager to hear it.

My opinions have changed, but not the fact that I am right.

Most of my faults are not my fault.

My objective is to save the world, while still leading a pleasant life. [2]

In the first half of life, the archetypal force that is my own is bright and real. Whether it is fulfilled or unfulfilled, I am convinced of my personal standpoint and convinced that it is eternally valid, no matter what other people might say or do. We have given examples of this conviction in earlier chapters where we talked about people who, while living out their own Great Story, fail to acknowledge the legitimacy of other archetypes than their own. This is one expression of the false assumption that we can clearly

ARCHETYPES
ARE INBORN
ORIENTATIONS
THAT
CALL
FORTH OUR FREEDOM
IN THE
CAUSE OF ACTIVE
SELF=
DETERMINATION

see the reality of those who are close to us. What we tend to do in fact, especially in early adulthood, is to see others only in the light of our own Great Story.

If Roger Gould is correct, this will be a natural tendency for any person in the first half of life. What any of us considers to be the "right" course or the "right" ideals or the "right" principles of behavior is bound to be shaped by our archetype. Each archetype has its own unique view of the right course to take, and our early lives are generally governed by the assumption that there is one right way to do things. It is therefore inevitable that in early adulthood, consciously or unconsciously, we show distinct favoritism toward the ideals and principles of behavior that flow from our own Great Story. This is why, as Chapter 7 explained, opposite archetypes are initially threatening or antagonizing to each other. It is only as we experience this antagonism that we gradually awaken to our prejudice toward the ways of being and doing that characterize our own archetype.

We stated earlier that no one finds identity and fulfillment in more than two archetypes. At this point it should be clear why this is so. For people who live out of two archetypes, one archetype is personal and the other is non-personal. (We discussed this distinction in the last chapter.) Any person's third and fourth archetypes are therefore opposite to their first and second archetypes, representing opposite attitudes toward the personal and non-personal worlds.

I can appreciate the qualities of people who live opposite stories to my own. I can even get a better assessment of my own strengths and deficiencies. But I can't find *identity and fulfillment* in the two archetypes that are opposite to mine. I can recognize the values and the outlook on life that belong to my opposite archetype. Indeed the normal course of life demands that I engage in a good many of the activities that belong to my opposite archetype. But the activities and attitudes and values that are most natural and spontaneous to my opposite archetype will never be as *natural* and *spontaneous* to me.

In fact, it is dangerous to spend the greater portion of our days and weeks in activities that are not connected to our Great Story. If we are unable to bring the gifts of our preferred archetypes to bear on our job or on the tasks which occupy most of our waking hours, we will quickly begin to experience disorientation, stress, anxiety, resentment, boredom, envy. We will feel fragmented and cut off from something that is essential to our well-being. People who are not in touch with their Great Story will be playing roles much of the time. This makes them prime candidates for midlife burnout.

Maturity therefore does not mean that we look in new directions or try to live a story that is opposite to what we have lived in the first half of life. Look once more at the short cameos of the eight archetypes a few pages back. None of them suggest that you have to make your opposite archetype part and parcel of your personal identity. This would be an impossible task. Rather, integration of opposites means that the dark or unconscious or undeveloped side of *your own archetype* has to be integrated with what is bright and conscious and developed. This is the "integration of opposites" which each of the cameos describes.

Throughout this book we have pointed out the similarities between the parallel masculine and feminine archetypes. Mother has much in common with Father, the Amazon with the Warrior. Seeker and Companion are similar, and so are the Sage and the Mediatrix. It is almost as though there are ultimately four Great Stories, not eight. To satisfy the demands of theory—and any theory should be consistent and coherent—each of the pairs of archetypes (Father-Mother, Warrior-Amazon, Seeker-Companion, Sage-Mediatrix) can be thought of as male and female incarnations of four larger archetypes which transcend the sexes. These over-arching archetypes remain nameless because they are sexless: we can't talk about real people who live real stories unless we take gender into account. However, there are some things we can say about men and women in general, whatever their particular archetypes might be.

There are two principles, in both men and women, which influence women and men in somewhat different ways. Earlier we referred to these principles as "focused consciousness" and "diffuse awareness." Let us go back to these concepts and see what they entail.

FOCUSED CONSCIOUSNESS	DIFFUSE AWARENESS
reason	receptivity
mind	relatedness
thought	feeling
disciplined meaning	awareness of the whole
analytic	synthetic
produces civilization	produces wisdom
Logos	Eros

Two other terms can be added to these columns, namely "masculine principle" in the left column and "feminine principle" in the right. Focused consciousness is like seed which fertilizes the soil, the receiving earth of diffuse awareness. In many medieval paintings of the Annunciation, the Logos or word of God is represented as a shower from the heavens penetrating the womb of the virgin Mary. Early Christian writers spoke of the human soul as the fertile womb which is made to receive the word, so that every person who listens to the word becomes the mother of God giving birth to the word of God.[3] The art and imagery of ages past often evokes the idea that you and I, man or woman, male or female, carry within ourselves both the masculine and the feminine.

But times change. This kind of imagery is not fashionable today. Many educated people argue that all sexual role differences are purely cultural, and that in their essential psychology male and female are the same. It is not possible to resolve this question scientifically because it is not yet known exactly where physiology leaves off and cultural influences begin. Ken Wilber offers what we think is the most helpful way to theorize about man-woman differences.

In his book *Up from Eden*, Wilber suggests that we should distinguish between male and female body, and male and female mind. From all that the science of physiology tells us, it seems clear that there are some basic psychological consequences to being male or female. It appears that the male and female *body* are "wired" toward just those sex differences that are caricatured as the stereotypical male (active, aggressive, assertive, et cetera) and the stereotypical female (passive, non-aggressive, emotional, et cetera). But the human *mind* is a different story. To the extent that the mind can transcend its initial embeddedness in the body, the mind tends to transcend the sexual differences that are rooted in our physiology. The more male and female grow in consciousness, the more they discover a mental equivalence and a balanced identity.[4]

Less mature individuals tend to display the stereotypical attitudes of their particular sex. Developed personalities, on the other hand, tend to be mentally androgynous. In this frame of reference, we can comfortably speak of focused consciousness as the "masculine" principle in both men and women, and diffuse awareness as the "feminine" principle in both women and men. (We could also refer to these opposite principles as black and red, or dub and flub. But then we would cut ourselves off from the imagery of past ages, where the ideas of "masculine" and "feminine" evoke something larger than a man and a woman. Typically masculine and typically feminine images in ancient art and literature, and much modern art and literature as well, are usually *symbols* of focused consciousness and diffuse awareness.)

Recent research shows that the most developed personalities

display a balance and an integration of both principles. In other words, the more you grow in self-awareness, the less you are stereotypically male or female. Or as Saint Paul put it, evoking Christ as a figure of the totally whole person, "in Christ there is neither male nor female."[5]

FOCUSED CONSCIOUSNESS	DIFFUSE AWARENESS
reason	receptivity
mind	relatedness
thought	feeling
disciplined meaning	awareness of the whole
analytic	synthetic
produces civilization	produces wisdom
Logos	Eros
'MASCULINE'	'FEMININE'

These two principles are opposite but complementary. People who exhibit the qualities of only one of these columns are likely to be immature and stereotypical males or females. In each one of us, male or female, the masculine needs the feminine and vice versa. If it is not balanced by the feminine principle, focused consciousness will lead a man into rigid and dessicated rationalism. A woman whose diffuse awareness is unbalanced by the masculine principle will find herself mired in confused and mushy sentimentality. For any woman or man, the integration of the opposite principle, masculine or feminine, is the work of a lifetime.

Ordinarily it is not until the second half of life that we can turn our attention to this particular facet of integration. During the first half of life, men and women alike have the task of making firm contact with the principle that is closest to the "body-wiring" of each sex. Males usually establish contact first with the masculine principle, and females with the feminine principle. Mature personalities will go on to transcend sexual and physiological

differences, but this can be done only when the psychic orientation that is naturally connected with one's sex is well integrated.

Men and women therefore approach the goal of integration
and maturity from different directions:

Diffuse awareness, the feminine principle, is a woman's special gift. If she has developed it well in the first half of life, her
diffuse awareness is an active awareness, not passive and not unconscious. She has a sense of the wholeness of things, how everything in the world is connected, and she can offer to men the
wisdom of the prophet and the artist. In the second half of life,
her task is to explore the world of focused consciousness, the masculine principle. She will center in on specific interests and is-
sues, looking more closely, more analytically, and with more
discernment at things which have interested her in a general way.
She may involve herself in social or political causes, taking up a
new career. As she becomes more focused, she often develops an
incisiveness that is a marvel to the men around her.

Focused consciousness, the masculine principle, is a man's
special gift. If he has developed it in the first half of life, he has a
fine analytic sense of what the parts are that make up the whole
of anything. He knows how to look at them one by one, take them
apart and analyze them and explain what they mean. He can offer
to women focus and disciplined meaning, scientific discovery,
and the productions of civilization. In the second half of life, his
task is to open himself to the world of diffuse awareness. Hobbies
will often be a means for expanding his focus. He will broaden his
interests more and more beyond the concerns of his profession,
and will even lose interest in the things which at one time totally
occupied his attention. As he acquires a greater sense of the
wholeness of things, he often develops a sensitivity that is a marvel
to the women around him.

These are very general descriptions which individual men
and women live out in their own unique ways. The descriptions
are enough to indicate that although men and women share the

same essential goal of integration and wholeness, the *psychic flow of life* is not the same for the two sexes. Women and men have different psychic tasks in the two halves of life, and the difference cannot be reduced simply to cultural conditioning or the roles that society expects of each sex.[6] At the same time, we have observed in our work with archetypes that some men and women get in touch more easily with their opposite principle.

Among the four feminine archetypes, *Amazons have the most ready access to the masculine principle*. The Amazon's way of being and doing depends heavily on focused consciousness, and so Amazons tend to develop this principle earlier than do other women. In fact, some Amazons have to make a conscious effort not to lose touch with their feminine principle. They need to pay attention to the qualities of diffuse awareness and actively develop them. Some Amazons seem to fall into the grips of the masculine principle, and in this case they constantly exhibit the stereotypical traits of assertiveness and aggressiveness which are associated with the masculine principle. The fact that the Amazon has the most ready access to the masculine principle does not mean that she has consciously integrated it.

The Mediatrix is opposite to the Amazon. We talked earlier about the vagueness and lack of focus which is characteristic of this archetype, and how most mediumistic women do not seem to find their place in life until they are older. The Mediatrix by definition has the most difficulty getting in touch with the masculine principle. Focused consciousness is more distant from her way of being than it is from any other archetype. And yet it is the masculine principle which finally rescues her. It is only as she develops ways of focusing herself that the Mediatrix comes to find fulfillment in her Great Story.

Among the masculine archetypes, *Sages have the most ready access to the feminine principle*. This is often observable early in life. In childhood as in adulthood, Sages tend to be the least interested in the competitive and aggressive activities that are characterized as "macho." Sometimes Sages appear effeminate to other males, and indeed if they are in the grips of the feminine principle they are likely to exhibit the stereotypical traits of passiveness and emotionality which are associated with that principle. In our basic description of the Sage in Chapter 3, we mentioned how important it is for the Sage actively to develop his inner feminine if he is to find fulfillment in his archetype. The fact that the Sage has the most ready access to diffuse awareness does not mean that he has consciously integrated it. If he does not develop it in a conscious way, he will fall prey to its dark side.

The Warrior is opposite to the Sage. The qualities of diffuse awareness are more distant from his way of being than from any other archetype. He is not likely to see much value in those qualities until he is quite mature. More than any other masculine archetype, Warriors tend to be driven by the desire for accomplishment to the point where they burn out and become brittle, blaming other people for their own lack of fulfillment. Just as the Mediatrix is finally rescued by her inner masculine, so is the Warrior saved by contact with his feminine principle. As he integrates within himself the qualities of diffuse awareness, the Warrior develops wisdom and a sense of how everything belongs to a whole. This wisdom, which goes beyond mere knowledge, is more difficult for the Warrior than for any other archetype.

The masculine and feminine principles involve different ways of being aware of the world, and hence they have to do more directly with the a-personal archetypes than with the personal archetypes. Still, some generalizations can be made about the remaining archetypes. In our experience, Mother is likely to be more in touch with the masculine principle than is the Companion. The Seeker has more ready access to the feminine principle than does Father. But it is important to remember that the archetypes appear in different configurations. Thus, Warrior-Seeker is likely to get in touch with the feminine principle more easily than Warrior-Father. Mother-Amazon usually has better access to focused consciousness than does Mother-Mediatrix. Here as in other cases, one's second archetype has important consequences.

Early in the 1930's Jung compared the two halves of adult life to morning and afternoon. In his essay, which was among the first things written about the midlife transition, Jung wanted to make the point that each stage of life has its own distinct meaning. "A human being would certainly not grow to be seventy or eighty years old if this longevity had no meaning for the species to which he belongs. The afternoon of human life must also have a significance of its own and cannot be merely a pitiful appendage to life's morning."[7]

We are now used to the idea that each period of life has its own particular psychological tasks. But translating this idea into a lived reality is not easy for everyone. Movies and advertising and TV dramas still favor the looks, the clothes, the stamina, and the desires of the morning of life. Our culture makes it difficult to resist the feeling that life after midlife is a mere "appendage" to life's morning. If we give in to this attitude, we pay for it with damage to our souls. The evening of life which is old age will be a still more pitiful appendage. "We cannot live the afternoon of life according to the program of life's morning—for what was great in the morning will be little at evening, and what in the morning was true will at evening have become a lie."[8]

Maturity, the integration of opposites, is the particular task which begins with the afternoon of life. If one embraces this task in the afternoon, then the evening of life is likely to be a time of great peace and wholeness.

The Great Stories help us to understand the wholeness which is the goal of life. We need more than ego identity, the development of our skills, and roles that suit us. Whenever it is that a person may accomplish these goals, they are still the goals of life's morning. The afternoon of life draws us to something more, something deeper, something other. In all of us there is a yearning to experience ourselves as individuals who are unique and yet part of a whole. The enduring philosophies and religions along with the great literature of the past and present suggest that this yearning is not just a desire but in fact our human destiny. We need to belong to something larger than ourselves, and our personal stories include responsibility for being part of a whole.

The archetypes offer us a sense of belonging to a whole. The Great Stories make us aware of our participation in a mystery that is even greater than the mystery of our own personal uniqueness. As we explore our archetypes and bring them to consciousness, we are caring for our personal destinies and at the same time contributing to the whole and facilitating its becoming.

Notes

1. Roger Gould, *Transformations: Growth and Change in Adult Life* (Simon & Schuster, 1978).
2. Ashleigh Brilliant, *I May Not Be Totally Perfect, But Parts of Me Are Excellent* (Woodbridge Press, 1979), *passim*.
3. E.g. Meister Eckhart, who echoes Jerome and Origen in his sermon 88, "The Virgin Birth" (ed. Pfeiffer I, 221–222).
4. Ken Wilber, *Up from Eden* (Doubleday, 1981), pp 228–231.
5. Galatians 3:28.
6. Those who are familiar with Jungian psychology might wonder why we have not used his concepts of "anima" and "animus" to describe the difference in orientation between male and female psychology. Jung's own use of these terms sometimes confused the archetypes of masculine-feminine with the culturally conditioned roles of male-female. It was half a century ago that Jung introduced the concepts of "anima" and "animus" to the psychological world, in an effort to clarify the differences between men and women. He should not be blamed for failing to make distinctions which are easy to make half a century later. It is unfortunate that today, outside of Jungian circles, the terms "anima" and "animus" seem to convey stereotypes which Jung would never have intended. This book owes much to Jung's

seminal work, but for the reasons mentioned here we have chosen not to bring his terminology of "anima" and "animus" into our discussion of the masculine and feminine archetypes.

7. C. G. Jung, "The Stages of Life," in *Modern Man in Search of a Soul* (Harcourt Brace; first published in 1933), p 109.
8. *Ibid.*, p 108.

Appendix

ARCHETYPES AND THE MBTI

istj amazon-companion

My archetype
helps to tell me why
i am quite different
from others who are the
same psychological type
as myself

How do the masculine and feminine archetypes relate to Jung's theory of psychological types and the Myers-Briggs Type Indicator (MBTI)? The pages that follow will be of interest to the many people whose lives have been enriched by an understanding of psychological type. This Appendix presupposes that the reader is familiar with the work of Isabel Briggs Myers and the basic concepts and terminology of the MBTI.[1]

We have worked with over two thousand people in courses from two to four days in length. The first part of the course includes a thorough explanation of type theory. The basic explanation of types, which takes three or four hours, is given *before* the results of the Type Indicator are given back. This method offers participants the opportunity to understand type theory, step by step: the Judging-Perceiving preference, the Extravert-Introvert preference, and so on. As the explanation proceeds, participants are asked to name their preference on each of the MBTI scales. When they are finally given the results of the MBTI, nine out of ten people find that they have named their preferences exactly as the Type Indicator did. Where there is a discrepancy, it is usually because of the person's *archetype*, as we shall explain below.

In the second part of our course, after the participants have worked through the MBTI types and have come to understand the implications of the types, we present the archetypes. We tell the Great Stories, much as they are given in Chapters 2 and 3. It is up to the participants to name their own stories.

We do not have an "archetype indicator" other than the reflective questions which appear in Chapter 4. It would be difficult to create an item pool which would differentiate between the archetypal *activities* in which one is involved and the total *story* in which a person finds identity and fulfillment. One of the benefits of listening to the Great Stories and discerning one's archetype on the basis of the questions in Chapter 4 is that people can distinguish their archetype from the activities in which they are engaged. For example, it is a great relief for a Sage who happens to spend much of his working day in Warrior activities to recognize his own Great Story. In any case, with some reflection, nearly all of our participants are able to name their archetypes with confidence.

Participants in our courses consistently remark that the archetypes have answered important personal questions which the MBTI left unanswered. The following pages will show how the archetypes complement the MBTI types, taking account of significant aspects of personality which type theory does not and is not meant to explain.

The generalizations we shall make here are based not on theory, but on our actual experience with people. From the viewpoint of theory, it is tempting to look for a direct correlation between the four functions in type theory—thinking, feeling, sensing, intuiting—and the four archetypes, masculine or feminine. At least one writer has jumped to this conclusion, identifying each of the four functions with one of the archetypes.[2] When we began our workshops on type and archetype in 1981, we asked ourselves whether there might be any such correlation. For example, are most Seekers and Companions P's rather than J's? Are most Mediatrixes intuitive rather than sensing? Is there a consistent link between any of the Great Stories and some facet of psychological type?

For several years we collected data from the participants in our workshops, and we reported this data in an article in the *Journal of Psychological Type*.[3] At that time, having worked with some five hundred people, we were not able to observe any consistent correlation between type and archetype. Now, after working with four times that number, we are confident that there is no significant correlation.

Any archetype can be any psychological type. This is an observation from our experience with people, and it has led us to sharpen our ideas about the different aspects of personality that are unfolded by psychological types on the one hand, and by the Great Stories on the other. In Jungian terms, as we understand them, the MBTI psychological types are primarily expressions of the *personal* unconscious. The types have to do with inborn traits which are responsible for the way our energy flows, outward or inward (E or I), and the way we gather (P) and organize (J) everyday information in a variety of perceiving and judging ways (S or N, T or F).

The Great Stories deal with the larger reality within which we exercise, realize, or concretize our psychological type. The archetypes have to do with lifestyles, the myths we live, the larger stories that shape our lives and give them an overarching direction. In Jungian terms, the archetypes flow from the *collective* unconscious. This is where our personal stories plug into the Great Stories of the Hero, the Mother, the King, the Amazon, and all of the archetypes which we have described in this book.

Our work with archetypes has made us appreciate the accuracy of Isabel Myers' descriptions of the sixteen psychological types. Myers' own descriptions are tantalizingly brief and genderless, and they invite further research. However, in expanding her original descriptions, theorists should be cautious not to confuse type with archetype by identifying certain archetypal qualities with certain types. For example, many users of the MBTI have observed that ISFP's have difficulty developing a strong self-image. We have found this to be true of Sages and Seekers, Companions and Mediatrixes of that type. But most Amazons and Warriors who are ISFP's are confident, adventuresome, and have a strong sense of who they are. ENTJ men who are Warriors might exhibit characteristics that evoke the image of the Field Marshal.[4] But ENTJ Sages find it hard to identify with this description, which confuses type with archetype. If some men have difficulty with this description, imagine how baffled an ENTJ Mediatrix is to see herself described with a masculine and military metaphor.

Some type theorists have speculated that children's choices of toys and patterns of play are related to their psychological type. Type might be a factor here, but archetypes provide a more immediate explanation of children's play habits. The young Sage, for example, is more interested in conjuring tricks or in playing detective than is the young Warrior, who is more likely to collect knives or pictures of sports heroes.

There has been much speculation and writing about spirituality and prayer as related to type.[5] In our experience, archetype has as much to do with a person's spirituality as does type. A Seeker and a Father who are the same type will not be inclined to express their spirituality in the same way. Father is more likely to be comfortable with traditional forms of religion than is the Seeker, who often feels confined by conventional forms and religious authority. A Mother and a Companion, even if they are of the same type, will have different spiritual and prayer needs. (The way one spontaneously prays is influenced by the personal archetypes rather than by the impersonal archetypes, since prayer is a personal way of relating.)

Confusion between type and archetype does not appear in Isabel Myers' own work, which is carefully confined to the characteristics of *type*. Her type descriptions are genderless and do not contain exclusively masculine or feminine metaphors. Nor do her descriptions intrude onto the ground of the collective unconscious and the Great Stories. Myers' treatment of type upholds the observation we made above: Any psychological type can be constellated in any archetype, and there is no single archetypal pattern which is typical of any single MBTI type.

Chapter 9 mentioned how psychological theories are "templates" which we lay over human experience in an effort to understand it and name it. Type and archetype are two such theories, two templates that complement each other remarkably well.

Psychological types and the MBTI help to explain *how* we communicate.

Archetypes, the Great Stories, help to explain *what* we communicate.

Type and archetype are therefore different, and at the same time complementary. The MBTI psychological types name the basic ways in which we communicate our thoughts and feelings and values. The archetypes, which give an account of the underlying mythical trends that shape our lives, explain the source of our energy and motivation. What makes for *meaning* in life comes mainly from our archetype, not from our type.

This is why people of the same psychological type can be disruptive to each other. For example, an NF usually understands quite readily what another NF is saying. But if one NF is an Amazon and the other a Mediatrix, the message can lead to argument and conflict because of the difference in personal values coming out of the different archetypes. These two women communicate in the same way, but they are energized in opposite ways. Two ST males communicate easily enough, but if one is Father and the other is Seeker, sparks are likely to fly.

Two persons of a similar type communicate their differences easily. But *what* they are communicating so clearly may be a difference in archetypes, and therefore a difference in values. For example, because of their different values, people of different archetypes will be inclined to spend money for different reasons. Two people who are similar in type might constantly find themselves arguing over finances. The disagreement will be communicated as clear as a bell because of the type similarity. But the *source* of the disagreement lies in differing archetypes.

Married couples whose MBTI types are different often have difficulty explaining themselves to each other. But opposite *types* often find a source of harmony and communication when they live complementary *archetypes*. For example, an ISTJ husband who is a Father and an ENFP wife who is a Mother weather their storms because their archetypes mesh. They are living a similar story and pursuing the same values.

Conversely, spouses who are the same psychological type can have severe marital difficulties because their archetypes are opposite. Take for example the INFP Companion who is married to an INFP Father. The different archetypes they are living (or want to live) can represent opposing values and very different attitudes toward parenting.

Parent-child differences seem to work in a similar way. A daughter who is an intuitive (N) Companion will very likely get more compassion from a parent who is a sensing (S) Companion than from one who is her same type (N) but whose archetype is Mother. A sensing (S) Warrior is likely to understand his intuitive (N) son who is also a Warrior, more easily than he understands his other intuitive (N) son who is a Sage. When all is said and done, a difference in *archetypes* between parents and children seems to cause more conflict than a difference in *types*. The reason, again, is the strong difference in personal values that are embodied in opposite archetypes. This difference will begin to make itself felt in the family when the child is still very young.

People's *archetypes* are usually more obvious and more immediately noticeable than their psychological *type*. This becomes all the more true as we get older and more settled in our Great Stories. Chapter 7 described how we seem to "wear" our archetype in public without even intending it. When meeting someone new, and before many words have been spoken, we pick up positive vibrations from a person who is living an archetype similar to our own: there is a sense of the familiar. We pick up negative vibrations from our opposite archetype: there is an immediate wariness. Different psychological *types* affect each other more subtly, and there usually has to be more verbal communication before type differences become very noticeable.

A person's archetype can be so overriding that it is misleading in relation to the MBTI types. This is especially true for Amazons and Warriors. Many F's who are Amazons or Warriors tend to think they are T's. This happens because some of the personality traits of these archetypes (self-contained, independent, task-oriented) are easily confused with the qualities of thinking types (objective, impersonal, analytic). INFJ Amazons and Warriors often seem to be not only E but T. In this case the J combined with the archetype makes for an extraverted thinking appearance.

On the other hand, Seekers and Companions who are T's seem less T than thinking types who are Warriors or Amazons. Seekers and Companions who are J's often appear to be P's, given the nature of their archetype. The J Mediatrix invariably looks like a P.

Archetypes help to clarify the confusion that many people experience regarding extraversion and introversion. I's in particular often name themselves as E's. In our experience, these are usually Warriors and Amazons who confuse their introversion with their archetype. Their orientation toward managing the outer world, and often their ability and success in doing so, convinces them they must be extraverts. This is one of the most common cases where an understanding of archetypes is essential for clarifying what the MBTI indicated—very correctly—about the person's type.

Archetypes also help us to avoid stereotypes of extraverts and introverts. One of the items in the MBTI (#7) asks for a response to a common situation: When you are with a group of people, would you usually rather (a) join in the talk of the group, or (b) talk with one person at a time? The Indicator scores this as an EI choice. But we have found that almost all Companions and Seekers who are *extraverts* make the *introverted* choice in this situation: they prefer talking with one person at a time. The reason for this is that Companions and Seekers, introvert *and* extravert, prefer relating one-on-one rather than to groups.

Certain combinations of type and archetype can be quite overpowering. Warriors who are ST's, for example, are usually very capable and efficient. But an ST Warrior has to be careful about the way he manages power and people. His sensing-thinking orientation does not tend to assist him in developing values having to do with people and relationships. As we mentioned earlier, the Warrior is the man who most needs to develop strong personal values if he is not to be a cutthroat. Many Warriors are F's. This combination tends to offer a good balance. These same observations apply to many ST Amazons.

Often sensing Mothers and Fathers feel betrayed to find that the world is changing behind their backs. Mothers and Fathers who are sensing types are more inclined to "keep up appearances" than do intuitives of the same archetype.

Companions and Seekers who are P's, when relating to or working with J's who are Mothers or Fathers, will be inclined to adopt a "son" or "daughter" role. Perceiving Companions and Seekers can be mature people, but if they are not aware of this tendency they can easily lose the particular authority that belongs to their archetype.

Many of these examples suggest that type and archetype can have a "softening" or a "hardening" effect on each other. Here are some further illustrations of this point:

The intuitive Mother is not as preoccupied with social structures and preserving tradition as is the sensing Mother. The sensing Companion will be more attentive to the physical needs of the one she accompanies than an intuitive Companion would be.

Mothers and Fathers who are SJ's have more difficulty recognizing their dark side or what is undeveloped in themselves. NP Mothers and Fathers are not usually as rigid. On the other hand, Companions and Seekers who are NP's have difficulty recognizing and disciplining their undeveloped side. SJ Companions and Seekers are not as irresponsible as the NP's of their archetype, and they are usually more loyal in their relationships.

How people approach their professions depends heavily on the Great Story they are living. Their professional "style" comes from their archetype. How they *communicate* this style comes from their psychological type. In the area of teaching, for example, an ENFP Mother will have a different teaching style from a Companion of the same type. Mother experiences her class as a family or community, and she is preoccupied with the good of the whole. Companion on the other hand sees her class as a gathering of individuals with particular individual needs. An ISFP nurse who is a Mediatrix will have chosen her profession for reasons that would not motivate an ISFP Amazon.

An ISTJ insurance salesman who is Father will approach his clients in a different way from an ISTJ Seeker. Most managers are J's, but an ENTJ Sage will have a different management style from an ENTJ Warrior. In both of these examples, communication will be focused and decisive. But the motives and values which are communicated will not be the same.

Everyone who has been part of our workshops has been helped by the archetypes as a complement to the MBTI, but no one more than Mediatrixes and Seekers. Seekers have been comforted to learn that they can transcend the Eternal Boy syndrome, and that they have something of value to contribute to other people. Mediumistic women have felt most intensely, after working through their MBTI type, that something was missing, that some key element was left out of their type description. Recall that the Mediatrix is not inclined to have a strong ego. Knowing about the Mediatrix and her tendencies is very freeing for the mediumistic woman, whatever her type.

Although the Mediatrix is the most affected by the collective unconscious, do not assume that all women of this archetype are N's simply because the unconscious tends to be the province of the intuitive. We have met a number of sensing (S) Mediatrixes who suffer from much confusion emerging from the collective unconscious. Because their intuitive function is often undeveloped, S's have greater difficulty than N's in rising above the dark side of the Mediatrix. Sensing Mediatrixes who have not learned to trust their intuition often fall prey to superstitions, dire predictions, and dark forebodings.

Which comes first, the chicken or the egg, types or archetypes? In our experience, there is no better way to begin working with a group of people than with the MBTI. Pedagogically, it is much easier to start with *how* we communicate. But in courses that are oriented to personal growth and self-discovery, we find that type theory remains incomplete and somewhat too abstract if it is not complemented with the archetypes.

My Great Story is the source of my energy and values and motivation, and this gives *body* to my psychological type. My Great Story helps to explain why I act like an ISFJ or an ENTP in just the way I do. My archetype helps to tell me why I am quite different from others who are the same psychological type as myself.

Notes

1. The MBTI is used by many psychologists and vocational counselors as a tool for discerning people's basic interests and styles of communication. The theory behind the MBTI, along with many practical applications for relationships, communication, vocational choices, etc., can be found in the book which Isabel Briggs Myers wrote at the end of her life, *Gifts Differing* (Consulting Psychologists Press, 1980). The Center for Applications of Psychological Type, 2720 N.W. 6th Street, Gainesville, Florida, provides a bibliography of the extensive research which has been done on psychological type and its many implications and applications.
2. Betsy Caprio, *The Woman Sealed in the Tower* (Paulist, 1982), p 40.
3. Tad Guzie and Noreen Monroe Guzie, "Masculine and Feminine Archetypes: A Complement to the Psychological Types," *Journal of Psychological Type*, 7 (1984) 3–11.
4. David Keirsey and Marilyn Bates, *Please Understand Me* (Prome-

theus Nemesis, 1978), p 73. Keirsey's theory of temperament needs to take account of the difference between type and archetype.

5. The best article we have seen on the subject is by Robert Repicky, "Jungian Typology and Christian Spirituality," *Review for Religious*, 40 (1981) 422–435.